THE BASICS OF

ACHIEVING PROFESSIONAL CERTIFICATION
Enhancing Your Credentials

THE BASICS OF

ACHIEVING PROFESSIONAL CERTIFICATION
Enhancing Your Credentials

Willis H. Thomas, PhD, PMP, CPT

CRC Press
Taylor & Francis Group
Boca Raton London New York

CRC Press is an imprint of the
Taylor & Francis Group, an **informa** business

A PRODUCTIVITY PRESS BOOK

650.1 THOMAS 2014

Thomas, Willis H.

The basics of achieving
professional certification

CRC Press
Taylor & Francis Group
6000 Broken Sound Parkway NW, Suite 300
Boca Raton, FL 33487-2742

© 2014 by Taylor & Francis Group, LLC
CRC Press is an imprint of Taylor & Francis Group, an Informa business

No claim to original U.S. Government works

Printed on acid-free paper
Version Date: 20130430

International Standard Book Number-13: 978-1-4665-5456-6 (Paperback)

Library of Congress Cataloging-in-Publication Data

Thomas, Willis H.
    The basics of achieving professional certification : enhancing your credentials / Willis H. Thomas.
        pages cm
    Includes bibliographical references and index.
    ISBN 978-1-4665-5456-6
    1. Professional employees--Certification. 2. Occupational training. 3. Career development. I. Title.

HD8038.A1T46 2013
650.1--dc23   2013016488

Visit the Taylor & Francis Web site at
http://www.taylorandfrancis.com

and the CRC Press Web site at
http://www.crcpress.com

Contents

List of Figures

List of Tables

Foreword

In the United States, the term *professional certification* is frequently used as a catch-all term for several activities that apply to the credentialing of individuals. The lack of clarity has resulted in confusion when it comes to discussing credentials or designations that accompany a person's name. The number of new professional certification programs offered by professional associations (i.e., Project Management Institute) and professional organizations (i.e., for information technology) has increased astronomically, especially since the year 2000. It is believed that in the United States alone there are more than 3,000 designations (i.e., acronyms that become a suffix to a person's name) and the number of individuals pursuing professional certification from professional associations and professional organizations continues to rise. While it is hard to determine the exact number of professional certification worldwide, it is evident that growing popularity is not only in the United States.

- Professional certification has become the key to success for many professional associations and professional organizations.
- Professional association members (PAMs) have embraced professional certification.
- Professional certification has enabled many professional associations and professional organizations to define the required competencies to apply for and hold a job in specific industries.
- Professional certification is significant because it generates billions of dollars for the economy and thereby for those who provide products or services to the professional certification marketplace (i.e., certification exams, preparation materials, and add-on products and services associated with professional certification maintenance).
- Professional certification is a controlling force in employment and is becoming stronger.

This text is dedicated to those professional associations and professional organizations, professional certification recipients, and supporting resources that have made a commitment to creating and maintaining high-quality professional certification programs.

To certify or not to certify—that is the question. The job market has become increasingly competitive due to a number of factors, including

- Streamlined workforces due to mergers and acquisitions
- Consumer demand with an impact on the supply chain and thereby staffing requirements
- Nature of the virtual workforce and global market presence
- Revised job descriptions based on technical and behavioral competencies
- Competing demands for compensation aligned to value of the position

Many people are challenged not only with finding a job, but also keeping it. When a person comes to understand the importance of professional certification, it is deemed mission critical to job survival. Moreover, professional certification can instill a sense of self-worth and accomplishment, which creates job satisfaction and employee retention. Professional certification can be the difference between promotion and stagnation, employment and retirement, success and failure.

Although a college degree has become increasingly important, the need for professional certification cannot be underestimated. Often, the employer will value the person with a professional certification with a degree more than an individual with a degree alone. In some cases, professional certification may receive more recognition than a college degree. However, with the large number of professional certifications available, people and employers are many times confused about which path to take. It becomes a lifeline to those in professional networks who share similar interests and pursuits. This text explores the value of professional certification, which options will yield the best results, and how you can use professional certification to support the realization of your career aspirations. It focuses on professional associations and professional organizations headquartered in the United States and has extended application to those certifications on a global basis.

Acknowledgments

My goal in writing this book is to emphasize the importance of quality professional certification programs and to encourage those who are pursuing professional certification to thoroughly consider their options before making this very important investment and to encourage professional associations and professional organizations to work closer with organizations such as the Accrediting Board for Engineering and Technology (ABET), the National Commission for Certifying Agencies (NCCA), and the American National Standards Institute (ANSI) to continuously improve and mature their professional certification programs.

I would especially like to thank Jim Snyder of the Project Management Institute (PMI). Jim has been a long-time dedicated member of PMI. He was instrumental in its founding success. I became a member of PMI in 2002, became a PMP in January 2005, and completed my doctorate at Western Michigan University in 2008. For more than 10 years, I have been pleased with the professional certification process at PMI. Moreover, PMI was instrumental in supporting my educational initiative; my doctoral studies focused on project management and evaluation. I wrote my dissertation on project evaluation and lessons learned through the lens of meta-evaluation, a term coined by my advisor, Dr. Michael Scriven, in the 1960s. In October 2012, I received the Cleland Award from PMI for best publication in 2012 for the book, *The Basics of Project Evaluation and Lessons Learned*, which was an extension of my dissertation. I was able to meet in person with Jim Snyder twice in 2012 as I wrote this book. The picture (see page xvi) was taken at the global PMI Conference in Vancouver, Canada.

I also thank E. LaVerne Johnson, president and CEO of IIL. She has been an inspiration to thousands of people around the world who have achieved professional certification. Her commitment to excellence is outstanding.

I give special thanks to "some" of the many professional associations and organizations that strive to continuously offer and support high-quality certifications. The list is extensive, and includes such groups as:

- Association of Clinical Research Professionals (ACRP)
- American Health Information Management Association (AHIMA)
- American National Standards Institute (ANSI)

- American Society Association Executives (ASAE)
- American Society for Quality (ASQ)
- American Society for Training and Development (ASTD)
- Cisco
- National Organization for Competency Excellence (NOCA)
- Institute for Certification of Computing Professionals (ICCP)
- International Institute for Learning (IIL)
- International Organization for Standardization (ISO)
- International Society for Performance Improvement (ISPI)
- Institute for Supply Management (ISM)
- Microsoft
- Project Management Institute (PMI)
- Oracle
- SAP
- Society of Human Resource Management (SHRM)
- Society of Research Administrators (SRA)

Introduction

This book is a practical guide to professional certification. It will help you as the person seeking professional certification to understand the process and what goes on behind the scenes. It proposes to help those individuals pursuing professional certification programs (certificants) to make informed decisions about the options available and recommended processes to consider. It addresses professional certification offered by professional associations and professional organizations, such as a software company. It focuses on professional certifications that are based on job function and occupation. It targets professional certifications that are assessment based and developed by industry practitioners and leading subject matter experts (SMEs) who offer unbiased, third-party recognition of an individual's education, experience, skills, and abilities in areas such as

- Accounting and finance
- Communications and public relations
- Documentation/records management
- Education, teaching, training, and development
- Evaluation, measurement, and research
- Healthcare, hospital management, and pharmaceuticals
- Human capital management/human resources management
- Information systems/information technology
- Procurement management/vendor management
- Project, program, and portfolio management
- Quality and performance improvement
- Environmental health and safety
- Sales and marketing
- Supply chain management

The purpose for writing this book is support of professional associations and professional organizations and their professional certification recipients (past, current, and prospective) and of employers who are investing in professional certification. It is especially for people who are at a point of trying to justify professional certification, trying to determine whether it is worth the time and cost. It is for those individuals who need to move beyond having a "good gut feeling" about professional certification and need to make serious decisions on how to maximize their investment in professional certification.

The rationale for writing this book is that, based on my research, a similar book has not been written in quite some time. Some of the content in this book I was unable to find in other related books. Certification-related books that have been recently published address primarily the following content:

- A directory listing of professional associations and professional organizations that becomes outdated
- Specific subject matter in a functional area or discipline (i.e., purchasing)
- Exam preparation materials, including sample test questions
- Sales- and marketing-related material on how to apply for a certification
- Specialized information for voluntary professional certification (VPC)

Note: This book focuses on VPC and addresses the concept of mandatory professional certification (MPC). Those who are pursuing licensure or accreditation will also find practical application of this book. Moreover, those who are looking to use this text to achieve rewards and recognition, such as obtaining the much coveted Microsoft Valuable Professional (MVP) award will benefit from reviewing the content. As you read this text, you may become even more passionate about the topic of professional certification. It is intriguing and important to understand how the professional certification process works (or in some cases does not).

This text is not intended to be a sales tool for professional certification; however, after reading, the following may occur:

- You may ask yourself which certifications are worth pursuing.
- You may feel the need to stop procrastinating on that much-desired professional certification program.
- You may start inquiring how to put together an action plan to make professional certification happen.
- You may look at people around you who are in different places in their life and recognize that certification can begin early for some who have just graduated from high school and decide to pursue a career in information technology. You may also see it is the solution for others who have completed a terminal degree and want to reinvent themselves.

Chapter 1

Foundations

Key Lessons

- Professional Certification Defined
- How Does the Professional Certification Process Work?
- Why Is Professional Certification Needed?
- Who Needs Professional Certification?
- Where Should a Person Obtain Professional Certification?
- Which Path Should Be Taken to Achieve Professional Certification?
- When Should Certificate Programs Be Pursued?
- What about Qualification?

Professional Certification Defined

Professional certification as discussed in this book is a formal process by which an individual (personnel) is evaluated against an established standard. The individual must voluntarily apply for and earn a professional certification from a recognized professional association or professional organization to ensure the individual has the desired education, work experience, knowledge, skills, and abilities for the designated job function. The process for professional certification must adhere to industry standards and guidelines outlined by certifying agencies and should be recognized by the profession as a preferred method. Achieving professional certification requires meeting specified criteria, including the successful completion of an assessment and fulfilling continuing education requirements.

Professional certification results in the acknowledgment of a credential (or designation) to the individual (certificant). Professional certification as defined in

1

this text should not be confused with other forms of education for professionals, for instance, a company that independently certifies vendors (without an accrediting agency) to sell their equipment. While it is commendable that a company certifies salespeople to promote consistency and quality, many of these programs require growth and continuous improvement before they can be classified as certification and thereafter professional certification through industry acceptance.

Certification is a process that should represent best practice and support quality and compliance. Conformance to established standards is foundational to professional certification. Credentials attest to the person's knowledge or authority. A designation refers to the letters the individual uses after his or her name (i.e., Jane Doe, PMP, specifies that Jane Doe is a project management professional). These become the results of professional certification and are intended to identify those who have achieved professional certification.

Professional certification uses a formal process to acknowledge individuals who have met or exceeded an established standard. The reputation of the certifying agency (i.e., professional associations and professional organizations) determines how much the professional certification means to the occupation. Accordingly, those offering professional certification will usually request recognition by an outside agency that will attest to the professional certification meeting the standard. Usually, standards for professional certification include:

■ The affiliation or association with (i.e., becoming a member of) the certifying entity
■ The requirements to sit for the exam
■ The exam meeting accepted psychometric standards for exam development
■ The delivery of the exam (i.e., it is given at a testing center)
■ The scoring of the exam (i.e., some questions are not graded but used for other purposes)

Note: When a person says he or she does not need professional certification, the person should ask why that is the case. The answer may be legitimate, and that is OK. Just do not let it become an excuse.

Professional certification is a business and should be operated like one. However, professional certification is intended to be a voluntary process by which a nongovernmental professional associations and professional organizations recognizes a person who has met the requirements of the professional certification (Table 1.1). It is a credential that attests to an individual's (certificant's) understanding a specific body of knowledge (BOK). A BOK refers to the complete set of terms, definitions, concepts, and activities that make up a professional domain, as defined by the relevant professional associations and professional organizations.

There is sometimes confusion that results when professional certification is stated to be required for an occupation (i.e., in the job description, JD). In the

Table 1.1   Reasons to Pursue Professional Certification

Why I Should Become Certified	*Why I Should Not Become Certified*
It will increase my marketability.	It will take time away from my hobbies.
It will require that I stay current.	It will require that I spend time on it.
It will promote best practices.	I'm thinking … .
It will support effective networking.	I don't know.
It will help me realize my potential.	I would rather go fishing.
I will learn new things.	I don't have any excuse.

Figure 1.1   The range of voluntary professional certification.

real world, while professional certification should not be confused with licensure or accreditation, think of professional certification conceptually as voluntary up to the point they become mandatory (Figure 1.1). Is mandatory is still voluntary? Requiring professional certification has become a changing trend in the industry.

- Voluntary professional certification (VPC): "I decided to pursue it."
- Mandatory professional certification (MPC): "The position description states I must have it."

Here are some examples:

- **Required:** It becomes a must-have for the job. The employer might list Certified Six Sigma Black Belt (CSSBB) as required for a quality control auditor in the manufacturing area because of the complexity associating with root cause analysis. The JD may use the term *must-have* and may use it to disqualify applicants who do not currently hold the professional certification. In fact, the designation will be used to screen applicants into a category of qualified, and those who do not have it will not be considered.
- **Requested:** It becomes necessary for the project manager (PM) to complete PMP certification from the Project Management Institute (PMI). In this instance, there is perceived value that PMP designation will have direct

benefit to the employee and organization by helping them standardize PM processes according to the *Project Management Body of Knowledge (PMBOK Guide*, 5th ed.). In some instances, it may be necessary to complete the PMP certification within a specific timeframe after employment. In other words, continued employment, an increase in responsibility, or a promotion is contingent on obtaining and maintaining the PMP.

■ **Preferred:** It is beneficial for the organization to retain training and development professionals who have achieved the Certified Professional in Learning and Performance (CPLP) certification from the American Society of Training and Development (ASTD). In this instance, there is perceived value that CPLP designation will have a career benefit for the employee and improved performance for the organization. It may be handled in primarily one of two ways:
  – The CPLP preference may be used to qualify applicants. (*Note:* CPLP certification requires 3 years of industry-related work experience, passing a multiple-choice knowledge exam, and submission of a work product.)
  – The organization may put in the employee's professional development plan (PDP) for an objective to complete CPLP certification within a specific timeframe. This may be done by setting an annual growth objective for the position that requires completion of the CPLP certification within the calendar year. Completion of the certification may be linked to promotion or additional responsibility. Conversely, if a company has a performance improvement plan (PIP), this will work as well.

■ **Desired:** It is believed that having this professional certification will be a good addition. For example, the person is an internal junior recruiter who works on a team in human resources (HR). The person's job is focused on a specific area of HR (i.e., résumé reviews and initial interviews). The job advertisement states Society of Human Resource Management (SHRM) certification as PHR (Professional Human Resources) is a plus. The term *is a plus* is intended to convey it will be recognized as an accomplishment.

■ **Acknowledged:** This somewhat neutral category may use the term *noted*. In other words, the certification may or may not directly apply to the job. For example, the person has achieved Microsoft Certified Professional Developer (MCPD) certification. However, the person is moving into a new role within the quality assurance department and will perform totally new work as a validation specialist on an Systems, Applications, and Products (SAP) implementation. His or her certification may indicate his or her prior competence in a related information technology area but does not have direct relevance to the new position. Because it may or may not have instrumental use, the person will be required to obtain a new certification. As a result, the professional certification is only acknowledged.

■ **Unwanted:** A professional certification is unwanted when having a professional certification does not add any perceived value to the position or

Table 1.2 Examples of Behavioral and Technical Competencies

Behavioral Competencies	Technical Competencies
Achieving active listening	Managing projects
Taking part in team building	Designing training
Networking effectively	Installing hardware
Resolving conflict	Troubleshooting software
Negotiating	Performing validation
Influencing	Auditing documentation

may in fact be considered a disadvantage. This may occur under unique circumstances:

- The certified individual is working for a new software company. The person previously achieved software certification from a competitor that was also a software company. The two companies are rivals from a marketing perspective. It may be in the best interest of the person previously certified by the competitor not to list the current certification and to pursue a new certification that is recommended by the new software company.

Professional certification involves a professional development process focused on ensuring an individual remains competent in the job. We commonly refer to this as having competencies, which are personality traits and skills of the individual. There are two types of competencies: behavioral (art) and technical (science) (Table 1.2). We identify competencies using questionnaires and interview methods, such as the critical incident technique (CIT), which proposes to have an individual recall when a particular competency was demonstrated. Usually, these desirable personality traits and skills are refined into core competencies.

In the minds of many HR practitioners, realized competencies are a key attribute of organizational development. According to Barnhart (1997), organizations see professional certification as a natural outgrowth of quality and empowerment (Q&E). If this is true, then organizations investing in professional certification can realize improved employee performance. Some questions that surface are:

- What needs to be done to ensure there is positive return on investment (ROI) for professional certification?
- What are the measures of return, that is, the return on quality (ROQ)?
- What type of payback period is realistic?

Note: These questions are addressed in further chapters.

While competencies are the usual method of looking at personality traits and skills, it becomes interesting to ponder what other areas are worth considering regarding competencies. What came to me one day was a concept called SKATES:

- **S**kills: proficiency and expertise in the subject matter
- **K**nowledge: ways of knowing gathered through perception or learning
- **A**bility: potential, mindset, and willingness to be involved
- **T**alent: natural and innate ability to perform required activities
- **E**xperience: engaged interaction through observation or participation
- **S**ense: understanding that is common within the discipline or function

This is not to suggest that the term *competency* is an insufficient descriptor or that we need to invent another acronym. Rather, competencies many times need to be further decomposed to determine what we are really looking for in an individual to perform the job. The concept of SKATES is simply a method to further define competencies operationally.

Related to competencies is knowledge, and this should be looked at in two dimensions:

- Explicit knowledge: represents things that we can learn through training or education. It is codifiable. Proficiently executing specific tasks in computer software could be an example of explicit knowledge. Categorically speaking, people can generally transfer explicit knowledge.
- Tacit knowledge: refers to natural ability of the person. We gain knowledge through experience and observation and can do it usually through normal effort. It is a talent or innate, for example, singing or playing a particular sport. Because tacit knowledge is interpersonal, it is not easy to transfer: A person either can sing or cannot.

How Does the Professional Certification Process Work?

The professional certification process should be composed of a series of documented steps to ensure the applicant has met defined criteria before obtaining professional certification. Depending on the type of professional certification, there may be more steps required. For example, it may require multiple assessments, and each assessment may involve a series of activities, such as demonstrated work products. Some professional certification may be time phased and require agreed-on timeframes to progress to the advanced-level professional certification. For the most part, the process for professional certification is actually straightforward as illustrated in Figure 1.2.

In reality, professional certification can become complex, and completion is not an easy task. This is why so many people are asking the same question: "What do I need to do to become certified?" This is because each step of the professional

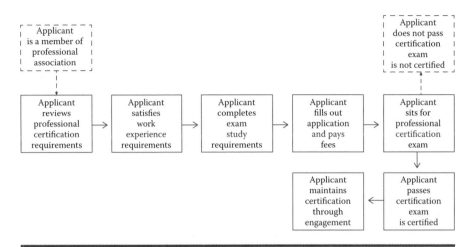

Figure 1.2 Typical professional certification process.

certification process requires the individual to understand what is actually required by the professional associations and professional organizations so the requirements can be met in an efficient manner.

Who provides input into the professional certification process? Input comes primarily from five sources:

- Professional associations and professional organizations (corporate management/board of directors)
- Accrediting agencies
- Third-party resources that create products or services to support professional certification
- Business partners
- Those who have been through the process and have been certified (certificants)

According to research conducted by the American Society of Association Executives (ASAE), the cost of marketing research can range between $30,000 and $100,000 or more. So, it is important that when professional associations and professional organizationss start the process of conducting research on whether it makes good business sense to offer a professional certification, they clearly understand the market. The question is: Will there be a demand for the professional certification? Professional associations and professional organizations that offer professional certification should be able to answer a number of important questions before offering the program:

- Where did the request for the certification originate?
- Has the audience for the program been identified (i.e., individuals or companies)?

- To what degree is the certification desired (i.e., beginning, intermediate, advanced)?
- To what extent is the certification desired (local, national, or international)?
- Who are the sponsors or key stakeholders who will endorse and support the program?
- Are there sufficient resources that can support the certification?
- What are the revenue projections for the certification?
- Who else is offering the certification?
- What is the long-term growth potential for the certification?
- When should the certification be offered (i.e., launch date)?
- How will certification materials be delivered to those interested in pursuing professional certification?

After a professional associations and professional organizations determines there is a valid need for the professional certification, it should select a consultant (business partner) who has experience implementing new professional certification programs. This process will become involved as the consultant is responsible for ensuring that all correct processes are followed, including working with organization, such as the Institute of Civil Engineers to establish the professional certification.

Assessment

The area of most concern when pursuing professional certification is usually the certification exam. It is important to clearly understand this term and the definition given to it by the professional associations and professional organizations. Exam fear is one thing, but people sometimes forget that the term *assessment* carries a different meaning in the world of professional certification. There are actually 10 possible meanings of the word *assessment*:

1. Education
2. Work history
3. Presentation of related work products (portfolio)
4. Test (multiple choice, true/false, yes/no, choose all that apply, drag and drop, matching, etc.)
5. Documented study hours, which is intended to confirm exam preparation
6. Demonstrated ability to perform the task
7. Attitude and behavior analysis (emotional intelligence)
8. Written examination (essay)
9. Oral examination (this can be performed through a panel of experts)
10. Quizzes using other senses (hearing, feeling, smelling, tasting, seeing)

What is involved in this assessment process? Who develops the tests? Why are the tests so challenging? The assessment development process involves a number of subject matter experts (SMEs) from the industry that have mastery of the subject content.

The professional associations and professional organizations should employ an expert in the area of testing and measurement. This individual is the psychometrician. Psychometrics refers to the measurement of an individual's psychological attributes, including the knowledge, skills, and abilities the person might need to work in a particular job. A psychometrician practices the science of measurement with a focus on jobs.

A psychometrician may have a graduate degree with a background in psychology. However, there is no formal degree that a person has to complete to become a psychometrician. The role of a psychometrician includes:

■ Serve on the committee to ensure effective and efficient implementation of assessments (i.e., oral exam, written exam, skill performance demonstration, etc.) and have input to administration policies for assessment to ensure accuracy, consistency, and fairness
■ Perform a job analysis or conduct a role delineation study to outline knowledge, skills, and abilities associated with the job
■ Define item writing guidelines for assessment and participate in the development of assessment materials
■ Configure assessment format (i.e., oral, written) to meet assessment objectives
■ Determine pass/fail criteria to ensure consistency with profession or occupation
■ Analyze assessment results using appropriate statistical methods
■ Establish scoring and reporting procedures and ensure the security and confidentiality of such scores and reports
■ Ensure the reported scores are reliable for the intended purpose of the assessment
■ Conduct ongoing research in the areas of reliability and validity
■ Attest to the test items as unique and not taken from another source

The Application Process

A second area that concerns prospective certificants is the application process. While they might have a chronological résumé, the documentation that is frequently needed for professional certification is a project-based reverse chronological résumé that details related project activities from the most recent, usually over the past 5 years. As the person puts together this information, there is a need to be careful of overlapping activities to avoid double counting of time periods.

Lack of Knowledge about Resources

A third area that may cause unnecessary stress is the lack of familiarity with available resources that can support an efficient and effective process of moving the professional certification forward to successful completion. In other words, some people who are seeking professional certification spend a significant amount of unnecessary time (as well as money) in pursuit of professional certification. Solutions are presented in further text for the concerns stated.

Certification Maintenance

After achieving certification, people are concerned about what they have to do to keep it; professional development units/continuing education units (PDUs/CEUs) represent a significant time and cost investment. It is estimated that maintaining certification can cost $1,000 or more per year. This is based on the requirement for an average of 20 PDUs/CEUs and association fees.

Ongoing Requirements to Stay Connected

A fifth area that may be unchartered territory is the need to stay connected to the professional associations and professional organizations and other certificants. This may require attending local chapter events, attending annual conferences, volunteering at chapter events, taking courses, participating on the board, documenting work experience, and more.

Why Is Professional Certification Needed?

Professional certification demonstrates a commitment to the occupation. Moreover, professional certification is intended to qualify an individual (and sometimes group) who meets or exceeds specific criteria (in some cases minimum standards) to perform the job. Examples include the following:

- Managing a complex project
- Implementing an integrated system to manage records
- Performing maintenance on computer hardware and software

The history of professional certification varies by industry, but comparatively speaking, the early 1980s were a major turning point for professional certification. For example, computer certification began in the mid-1980s. It was introduced by companies such as Microsoft and later by Novell. Many other forms of professional certification followed computer-related certification for a number of reasons:

- Computers and related technology are centrally important to certification programs.
- Electronic mail (e-mail) enabled communication from professional associations to their members, which provided an enabling platform for certification.

- Computers provide a means of accessing members on a global basis.
- Changes in the competitive global marketplace have increased the desire for obtaining professional certification.

When a person (or group) does not have the desired or required professional certification, the person may be unable to perform the work or may become out of compliance with the work performed. This creates a dilemma for the individual and business. It can jeopardize the reputation of the business and result in fines or lawsuits, especially in regulated industries. It can become even more complicated in dynamically changing workforces.

So, there is increasing rationale to support professional certification and to encourage employees to pursue it. One of the most effective ways to do this is through awareness and emphasizing the benefits of professional certification. Let employees know that keeping their skills up to date is advantageous for them and the business. Encourage them and recognize their accomplishments when professional certification is achieved and maintained. This can promote a positive attitude.

Because the nature of the workforce is continuing to change as businesses respond to the marketplace, there are increasing demands to do more with less. Mergers and acquisitions are an example of streamlining. Similarly, globalization that involves distributed workforces becomes another solution for downsizing in an organization. Moreover, changes in technology and ways of doing things have allowed many manual functions to be automated or eliminated, thereby putting people out of jobs as a result of downsizing. The terms *harmonization, integration,* and *standardization* are frequently used to describe these realignment-type changes.

When an existing position is eliminated, the person basically has three options if the person desires to remain employed by an organization:

- Leave the current organization and find a similar position with another organization
- Enhance personal credentials for a new position in the current organization
- Enhance personal credentials for a new position at another organization

When job change occurs, it is important to have an action plan that addresses what to do next. What to do next frequently involves looking at the need to enhance one's credentials through professional certification. This can sometimes appear to be a reinvention.

Reinvention should be a renovation or upgrade and not a demolition exercise. Reinvention is the process of conducting a skills assessment and outlining the roles and responsibilities a person is capable of performing. Before taking the next job, keep in mind that certification credentials are highly desirable. The certificant needs to have good intuition and to make sure the next job choice has the same in regard to ESP:

- **E**mployees: sufficient number of people on the team capable of doing the work
- **S**ystems: software and computers in place to ensure quality and compliance
- **P**rocesses: documented policies and procedures

Looking at a job as roles and responsibilities simplifies things by enabling a person to think of what he or she can bring to the next organization. In some cases, a JD will need to be adapted for some highly talented candidates. A JD may not adequately capture what the person is capable of delivering, and the individual may be overlooked during an interview because he or she did not exactly match the JD. A JD can include a road map of which professional certification becomes an integral part of the job. Reinvention puts the company in a better position to retain the employee by investing in retraining. Supporting certification efforts can help the employee perform better in the new assignment. It should be noted that retraining is an input to and output of professional certification.

Professional certification should be focused on maintaining professional certification and not just its initial achievement. Professional certification maintenance (PCM) requires ongoing learning and typically comes in the form of PDUs or CEUs. For example, the PMP certification issued by PMI requires 20 PDUs per year, which can be obtained by taking PM-related courses. The job status realization by the company and the individual is the REVEAL phase:

- **R**ecognize the current position may no longer be needed
- **E**valuate options for a revised/enhanced/new (REN) JD or new position
- **V**erify the REN position through job analysis
- **E**ducate the employee through retraining and certification
- **A**cknowledge the REN position with a formalized job offer
- **L**earn with a continuous improvement philosophy in the REN position

A key issue for the company and person is how to REVEAL effectively and efficiently (E&E):

- The context of effectiveness may concern how well the additional training and related certification meets the requirements of the revised JD.
- The context of efficiency may concern how much time it will take for the training and related certification.

The following practical approaches support the REVEAL process:

- Connect with associations that specialize in job analysis or role delineation studies, such as the SHRM, the Chartered Institute of Personnel and Development (CIPD), and ASTD.

- An outplacement service provides career consultation services that are usually paid for by the former employer. These companies are constantly conducting market studies and can give good advice.

The dynamics of the need for reinvention and the REVEAL phase should encourage the certificant to look at the new job opportunity (especially when external) as green, yellow, or red:

- Green light (go ahead): The company is seeking an experienced individual who has maintained professional certification to replace a member of management promoted to a new position. The interview process is straightforward, with no strangeness or hidden surprises, and it is a good match for the certificant and company to move forward. The certificant will realize a 20% increase in base pay and a 15% increase in possible bonus, which is based on performance. The position will have more responsibilities and may require location. The company has agreed to pay relocation expenses if the need arises for the person to move. The person who held the position previously has agreed to serve as a mentor for the new person coming in to provide for a smooth transition.
- Yellow light (caution): The company desires to hire an individual who has achieved professional certification, but several of the managers who have not achieved the professional certification are intimidated about this person's credentials. When the certificant expresses personal accomplishments, he or she feels as if these should not be stated. The person with the professional certification is regarded by several employees as an overachiever and people question if he or she will fit in. The interviews felt shaky, and the certificant is feeling uncomfortable about the job.
- Red light (stop): The position is brand new, and the company is looking to hire a person with professional certification in the occupation to hire employees, build systems, and establish processes. In the interim, no budget has been allocated, and the company expects the person with the professional certification will have the necessary skills and ambition to do it alone. The interview seemed extremely challenging, and the certificant is doubtful if he or she will be able to meet the high expectations. The certificant has a bad gut feeling.

Who Needs Professional Certification?

Professional certification is not a guarantee that the person will perform competently. Moreover, a professional certification earned 5 years ago is not a warranty on the job you hold today that may be partly the result of that professional certification. To address the question of who may benefit from professional certification, we need to know who may not benefit:

1. People whose roles and responsibilities do not directly involve job-related tasks associated with the professional certification.
2. People who have changed jobs, retired, and so on and their job functions no longer require the professional certification.
3. People whose knowledge clearly exceeds what the professional certification has to offer. If having the professional certification will be detrimental to a person's position or status because it is perceived to be for individuals at designated levels, then it would not be preferable to pursue the professional certification.
4. People who do not meet the current requirements of the professional certification. While this may seem to be an awkward response, a person who does not meet the requirement of the professional certification does not deserve it, although they may desire it and the organization wants it.

Professional certification is like a career vitamin, and the ongoing training required for certification maintenance is like exercise. Therefore, many individuals whose position can benefit from professional certification need it. Professional certification is not only for the benefit of the individual but also, more importantly, for the organization. The goal of professional certification is to maximize the investment in human capital. As Phillips (2002) discusses, a company should be able to realize the ROI from the employees it hires and develops. Similarly, an employee should become the best he or she can be in the position for which he or she was hired and come to realize full personal potential. How much an individual needs professional certification is entirely another question. Some of the drivers include regulatory or legal requirements to perform the work required. Each situation will be different.

If a person feels he or she does not need professional certification, the person should confirm that obtaining professional certification will not:

- Improve knowledge or understanding of the subject area
- Enhance his or her ability to do the job
- Require the person to keep up to date on changes or updates in related subject matter
- Increase the organization's effectiveness in the subject matter
- Set expectations of what employees should be doing with ongoing education

While many people pursue professional certification for an increase in salary or promotion, the nonfinancial benefits are sometimes just as significant. The scenarios are virtually endless, but frequently involve:

1. Empowering and motivating employees to increase job satisfaction
2. Enhancing the dynamics of internal relations through organizational learning
3. Planning for succession to prepare for continuous change

4. Increasing the organization's perceived value
5. Reinforcing conformance or compliance
6. Standardizing, integrating, or harmonizing initiatives
7. Promoting best practices
8. Improving competitive position
9. Making process improvement initiatives
10. Providing organizational growth and maturity

According to Christianson and Fajen (1998), professional certification is popular because it provides a current performance-based assessment of an individual's knowledge and skills. Most professionals will probably agree that they have considered their need for professional certification.

Professional certification consideration occurs at various points in one's life, such as relocation, promotion, revised JD, and change in reporting relationships. As one considers professional certification, it should encompass:

- Résumé or curriculum vitae (CV) review
- Visiting professional associations and professional organizations Web sites
- Reviewing professional associations and professional organizations trade journals
- Attending chapter meetings or conferences offered by the professional association
- Participating in forums offered by the professional organization

First, consider that a college degree may no longer adequately represent a person's career aspirations. This is due to a number of factors, including:

- When they received their first degree (i.e., bachelor's): Has it been longer than 10 years?
- Where they received their first degree: How is the educational institution ranked?
- Continuing education since the first degree: What courses have been taken?
- Limited focus of second degree (i.e., master's degrees like the MBA)
- Specialization of terminal degree: doctorates, law degrees, medical degrees, and so on

Second, a professional certification that closely aligns to a person's career objective may more accurately reflect the desired competencies (technical or behavioral) of the person's position. This is because:

- Professional associations and professional organizations establish JDs and therefore influence or set the standards for professional certification
- Those who have earned a professional certification want the standard to remain high

- Investments in human capital increase through professional certification
- The sociopolitical influence that exists due to professional certification is extremely strong because it employs many industries and generates billions of dollars in revenue

When should a person pursue professional certification? Each situation is different, but there is no time like the present to start working on a schedule or action plan for the desired professional certification. Even if the professional certification is more than a year off, put it in your next year's goals to readdress the need for the professional certification to help it become a reality. Here are some things to consider regarding timing:

- Does the person currently have what it takes for the professional certification? (may be termed E5):
  - Eligibility:
    - Education: college degree requirements
    - Employment: current need for the professional certification
    - Experience: history of related project completed
  - Economics:
    - Expense: Are they able to make the financial investment?
  - Energy:
    - Encouragement: support from family and coworkers
    - Enthusiasm: positive attitude
    - Endurance: commitment to remain focused
  - Ethics:
    - Essential: honesty and integrity required of the professional certification
  - Evaluation:
    - Exercises: resources to support training and preparation
- Examination: ability to pass the test

The question that each person pursuing professional certification must ask is, "Will I be better off in the long run after obtaining the professional certification?" The answer is usually yes.

Where Should a Person Obtain Professional Certification?

The best possible source is the preferred option for obtaining professional certification. Professional certification should be obtained from the professional associations and professional organizations that provides an affordable, accessible comprehensive program authorized by the sponsor (employer). It should also take into consideration any recommendations by governing bodies (i.e., regulatory agencies requiring the certification). The following criteria may aid in decision making:

- Reputation of the certification: What is the industry support for the certification?
- Number and type of people holding the certification (i.e., career level)
- When and why the certification was established
- Requirements to achieve and maintain certification
- Exam preparation materials and their sources
- Professional association support, including access to study groups and membership

Another concept to consider as it pertains to where to obtain certification is the type of certification:

- **Assessment-based certification:** Is the ability to pass a test (verbal, written, or hands on) the primary criterion for meeting the standard and earning the certification?
- **Competency-based certification:** Is it focused on the specific personality traits (behavioral competencies) or skills (technical competencies) to perform the work?
- **Education-based certification:** Is attending a series of courses that results in time invested the rationale for achieving the certification?
- **Experience-based certification:** Is experience the primary factor, with documentation of previous activities serving as the basis for certification?
- **Knowledge-based certification:** Is understanding how something functions such as navigation schemes in an application software program?

Which Path Should Be Taken to Achieve Professional Certification?

Applying for professional certification involves the processes associated with choosing the certification and completing the requirements (prerequisites) and associated paperwork. The path that one takes and the amount of time required to apply for professional certification depends on the type of professional certification. It is situation specific.

For example, one challenging decision regarding professional certification is whether to pursue levels of depth or diversify. For example, a director of HR is running many projects for a software company. The director is contemplating pursuit of a PHR professional certification and then obtaining the Senior Professional in Human Resources (SPHR) from the SHRM. On the other hand, the director wonders if he or she should obtain the PHR and bundle it with the

PMP professional certification from PMI. The director could also pursue the Agile Project Management professional certification because it has been reported to be the future methodology of the company.

Regarding the path that one chooses, it should be in line with career aspirations. The person should think about it in terms of these personal questions:

- "When I grow up" or come to the realization of the career I will be content with and the position I want to ultimately hold, what does it look like?
- Is it an existing position, or is it a position that will require a new JD to be created?
- If I want to be a PM, then should I pursue project management certification?
- If I am unsure of which path I should choose because I desire flexibility, then is it worth considering beginning with one certification the first year and plan on another one for next year?

The person will need to determine the correct path before he or she can answer the next question: "How long it will take?" Stating it another way, how long it takes depends on the path chosen. So, think of the professional certification process as an endeavor that might take some time to complete. It may take years to fully satisfy your longer-term plans.

Starting the process, on the other hand, can progress rather quickly. For example, to complete the professional certification process may take only a couple of weeks; in other cases, it can take more than a month. Many professional associations and professional organizations publish the upcoming examination dates so prospective applicants know when paperwork must be submitted. Paperwork may consist of:

- Application: usually the first step in the process
- Résumé or CV: provide detailed project-based version
- Portfolio: should include projects and achievements
- Letters of reference: should be from work sources or the professional network
- Transcripts: academic from educational institutions
- Certificate of course completion: for instance, PDUs

Considering that professional certification is frequently portable (can be transferred from one job to another), it can be used to increase the marketability of a person's credentials. It also makes it easier for a potential employer to find the desired candidate. Combining membership with the professional association affiliation is usually advantageous. However, it should be noted that the professional organization must be sensitive about having any mandate of the professional certification require membership and thereby annual member dues payments. This might be viewed as an illegal relationship. On the other hand, it is permissible for a professional organization to offer discounts associated with the professional certification to members.

When Should Certificate Programs Be Pursued?

For those people who choose not to pursue professional certification, another good alternative is a certificate program or professional certificate. Table 1.3 shows the difference between professional certification and certificate programs.

Some curriculum-based certificates may be regarded as professional certificates because they have more checks and balances in place, such as course prerequisites or assessments. Professional certificates may be priced higher, may take longer to obtain, and can be in greater demand.

According to ICE, an assessment-based certificate program is a non-degree-granting program:

- It has objectives that are focused in its design, development, and delivery (i.e., after completion of this training event, the participant will understand "X").
- It helps participants acquire specific knowledge, skills, or competencies.
- It involves an evaluation of the participants' achievement of the learning outcome.
- It awards a certificate only to those participants who meet the criteria, requirements, performance, or proficiency or pass the standard for the assessment.
- It is *not* a certificate of attendance or participation for attending a training event.
- It should not be confused with certification or becoming certified.

Table 1.3 Some Basic Differences between Professional Certification and Certificate Programs

Professional Certification	*Certificate*
Results in a designation to use after one's name	Listed on resume without a designation
Results from an assessment process	Results from completing course requirements
Has education requirements	Usually has no education requirements
Has experience requirements	Usually has no experience requirements
Has ongoing education requirements	Usually has no ongoing education requirements
Has standards set through credentialing authority	Usually has no credentialing authority standards

Examples of professional certificates include:

■ Project management:
  - PRINCE2* (Projects in Controlled Environments) Foundations: Verifies the project team member has sufficient understanding of the PRINCE2 methodology and can follow the established principles as a member of a project management team working within a supporting PRINCE2 environment. The foundation level is also a prerequisite for practitioner certification.
  - PRINCE2 Practitioner: Confirms the experienced practitioner has achieved sufficient understanding of how to apply and tailor PRINCE2 in a real-life application with the PRINCE2 environment.
■ Leadership development:
  - MIT Sloan Executive Certificates are awarded to participants who have completed at least four open enrollment programs within 4 years. Executive certificates are available in three focus areas and provide executives with the opportunity to customize their education plans.
■ HR management:
  - The certificate program in HR management addresses legal matters, staff recruitment, and development. It is intended to be part of the road map to HR certification from associations such as SHRM that offer the PHR certification.
■ Change management:
  - This certificate program involves organizational restructure, conflict resolution, mergers, acquisition, culture change, and related initiatives.

Now, let us look at how professional certification and certificates can complement each other. Those who achieve professional certification will still need to obtain certificates. Why is this the case? The following is the rationale:

■ **Certificate programs fill the gaps not addressed in certification programs:** For example, software is constantly updated to new versions. Each time complex applications are released (i.e., Microsoft Project), it is in the PM's best interest to attend training for the application and obtain the certificate.
■ **Many certificate programs can be used for PDUs/CEUs:** If the training is directly related to the professional certification, then PDUs/CEUs can be counted for maintaining the certification. In other words, by attending Microsoft Project training, the individual should be eligible to claim PDUs/CEUs for attending a full-day or multiple-day training session.
■ **Some good certificate programs are not certification oriented:** It is critically important to keep in mind that accredited certification programs are not the only good training out there. Many excellent programs will not invest the necessary time and cost to achieve accreditation, and it might not make

sense to do so. For this reason, ICE and other institutions have been or are now addressing the certificate program marketplace to reinforce the quality and standards for these initiatives.

■ **Maintain a flexible portfolio:** You do not want to appear to the employer as a certification junkie. In other words, it is not impressive to an employer to list credentials for the purpose having a long title that consists of many designations at the end of a person's name. For practicality, listing more than four designations is overwhelming (i.e., John Doe, PhD, PHR, CPIM, CPT, CQE). You will know when the number is too many when the name becomes lost in the number of certifications listed. Certificates are nice because they do not add acronyms to the title.

What about Qualifications?

Qualifications represent the individual's accomplishments that are in alignment with a specific position. Qualifications can be used to establish a standard and outline requirements for a job. This standard can detail direction to those interested in a specific vocation. So, what is the difference between qualified and certified (or qualification and certification)?

Sometimes, the distinction for qualification is not so well defined. It may have education and assessment requirements but may not be defined in terms of validity. Someone can be qualified but not certified or, conversely, certified but not qualified. This means that qualifications generally have to do more with a specific set of requirements to do a particular task or set of tasks, and certification may or may not sufficiently cover the expertise needed to be qualified for a specific job. Therefore, after certification has been achieved, it may not be surprising to see a qualification requirement. Table 1.4 presents a view of professional certification versus general qualification.

According to Manijack (n.d.), the advantages for qualification over certification are quicker time to market, cost, and convenience. This appears to be a U.S. perspective and does not appear to be the case as you examine how qualification is handled in other countries. For example, professional or vocational qualifications in the United Kingdom are subject to the European directives on professional qualifications and are usually awarded by professional bodies in line with their charters (Table 1.5). Most professional qualifications are chartered and follow on from having been admitted to a degree (or having an equivalent qualification).

The sector and type of professional qualification determine the length of time it will take to earn. Accreditation for professional qualification is provided by numerous professional bodies. Some examples include:

■ National Council for the Training of Journalists (NCTJ)
■ Chartered Institute of Marketing (CIM)

Table 1.4   Professional Certification versus General Qualification

Professional Certification	General Qualification
Is term used extensively in United States	Is term used extensively in EMEA (Europe, Middle East, Asia)
Represents high-stakes exams	Represents lower-middle stakes exams by comparison
Has proctored exams	May take advantage of nonproctored exams
Indicates engagement with certifying agency and accrediting body	Is managed internally without the engagement of certifying agency or accrediting body
Can be costly and time consuming	Is quicker and less expensive by comparison
Has validated approach based on industry input and best practices	Is a nonvalidated approach based on subject matter expert input
Is based on job analysis/role delineation study	Is not based on job analysis
Is legally defensible	Is not usually defensible
Is based on well-defined standards	Is based on good ideas or rough standards
Is based on methodology, knowledge, and understanding of what should be done	Focuses on ability to perform

- Institute of Civil Engineers (ICE)
- Royal Institution of Chartered Surveyors (RICS)
- Royal Society of Chemistry (RSC)

Professional qualifications can be a prerequisite to a promotion in the United Kingdom. Moreover, some professions require a certain level of qualification before the person can take the next step on the career ladder (Collett, 2007). Some consulting firms use professional qualifications as a recruitment tool. Deloitte, a globally recognized consulting firm, states the following on its professional qualifications Web site: "Whatever department you join, whichever exam course you undertake, you will benefit from working with a variety of client types and sizes and with some of the most experienced professionals in the country. The experience gained

Table 1.5 Professional Certification versus Professional Qualification

Professional Certification (i.e., in United Kingdom)	Professional Qualification (i.e., in the United Kingdom)
Can support hiring decision	May be required for hire
Can encourage promotion	May be required for promotion
Involves an accrediting Agency	Is chartered
Involves a certifying body	Involves affiliation with university or organization
Covers a wide range of occupations	Covers broad categories (i.e., consulting, auditing)
PDUs/CEUs must be earned	Training contract is signed
No exemptions are available	Exemptions available based on degree syllabus
Sometimes paid by employer	Many times paid for by employer
Usually one examination	May require multiple exams

in Deloitte will stand to you for life. We offer graduates the opportunity to pursue a number of professional qualifications."

At the end of 2011, the European Commission adopted a proposal for modernizing the Professional Qualifications Directive to make it easier for professionals to find skilled jobs across Europe. The European Commission introduced the European professional card to assist interested professionals in having increased visibility of their qualifications. For those individuals who work in European countries, it can be advantageous to obtain a professional qualification.

What about beyond Europe? The Australian Institute for Teaching and School Leadership (AITSL) is the designated assessment authority for early childhood (preprimary school) teacher, primary school teacher, and secondary school teacher occupations under the General Skilled Migration Program. The Assessment Subsidy for Overseas Trained Professionals (ASDOT) program provides support for those overseas trained professionals who may be financially disadvantaged. It provides financial support to cover the cost of assessments that must be successfully passed to qualify for employment in certain professions in Australia.

In a review of other countries that have requirements for a qualification, it can be seen as a common theme. Canada for example, utilizes a foreign credential assessment process to determine if the person meets the requirements for the position. It is also used for admission to colleges and universities. The "General Guiding Principles for Good Practice in the Assessment of Foreign Credentials" is the result of collaboration on the part of the Provincial Assessment Committee (PAC). PAC was in existence from 1996 to 1999. It then became the Alliance of Credential Evaluation Services of Canada (ACESC). The goal is to share information on assessment methods used across Canada, to establish good practice, and to identify common assessment principles.

Will there be more influence in qualification in the United States as in other countries? Will there be more influence in certification in other countries as in the United States since the late 1980s? It is a guessing game, but there is a good indication that qualification and certification (as well as certificates) will continue to have significant value throughout the world. One of the best ways to stay abreast of changes with respect to qualifications is to review job postings and look at the types of qualification and certification required for positions.

The whole discussion of qualification, certification, and certificates is still relatively young when you look at the history of the associations, companies, and agencies that have been established to support these forms of education. Some of the most challenging considerations are when certificants and those qualified to perform work across international borders choose to live in different countries. The best investment may be those qualifications, certifications, and certificates that have global recognition.

Suggested Reading

Barnhart, P. (1997). *The Guide to National Professional Certification Programs*, 2nd ed. Amherst, MA: HRD Press, CRC Press.

Canadian Information Center for International Certification. (n.d.). General Guiding Principles for Good Practice in the Assessment of Foreign Credentials. Retrieved February 4, 2013, from http://www.cicic.ca/502/good-practice.canada.

Cizek, G., and Bunch, M. (2007). *Standard Setting: A Guide to Establishing and Evaluating Performance Standards on Tests*. Thousand Oaks, CA: Sage.

Collett M. (2007). Guide to Professional Qualifications. Retrieved February 1, 2001, from http://www.jobs.ac.uk/careers-advice/careers-advice/947/guide-to-professional-qualifications.

Deloitte Global Services Limited. (2012). Professional Qualifications. Retrieved February 1, 2013, from http://mycareer.deloitte.com/ie/en/students/learning-and-development/professional-qualifications.

Edwards, J., Scott, J., and Raju, N. (2003). *The Human Resources Program-Evaluation Handbook*. Thousand Oaks, CA: Sage.

Manijack, P. (n.d.). Qualification versus certification. *Certification Magazine*. Retrieved February 1, 2013, from http://www.certmag.com/read.php?in=773.

Phillips, J., and Phillips, P. (2002). Technology's Return on Investment. *Advances in Developing Human Resources* 4, 512–532.

Project Management Institute. (2013). *Project Management Body of Knowledge*. 5th ed. Newtown Square, PA: Project Management Institute.

Techrepublic.com. Provides a significant number of white papers on information certifications.

Tittel, E. (2003). Rating certifications. *Certification Magazine* April.

Chapter 2

The Certification Marketplace

Key Lessons

- The Certification Jungle
- Milestones in Professional Certification
- Credentialing Authorities
- Centers and Institutes for Association Leadership
- Association Management Companies
- Business Partners and Consultants
- Professional Association versus Professional Organization
- Professional Association Governance and Membership
- Professional Organization Structure and Community Members
- Registered Education Providers
- Educational Institutions
- Employers
- Critics

The Certification Jungle

Certification represents one of the fastest-growing multibillion-dollar marketplaces that has engaged a multitude of businesses in an amazing race to offer a vast array of products in services as they strive to increase the value of human capital. One way to describe it is a jungle where people, vendors, and professional associations and professional organizations are swinging back and forth to make connections. Christianson and Fajen (1998) discuss the more than 300 certifications that were available for computer and network professionals, and that number has dramatically increased since the turn of the century.

Certification has resulted in increased job opportunities for the suppliers and recipients of certification. Professional certification has become a subset of the education marketplace. In other ways, it is apparent that professional certification is not a part of traditional education but rather is an entity of its own within a diverse professional development arena. professional certification has generated huge interest and thereby revenues, of which a significant part is classified as nonprofit or not for profit. The certification marketplace is sustained through:

- Credentialing authorities
- Centers and institutes for association leadership
- Association management companies (AMCs)
- Professional associations
- Professional association members
- Professional organizations
- Professional organization subscribers
- professional associations and professional organizations business partners and consultants
- Educational institutions
- Employers

The interrelationship explored in this chapter is depicted by Figure 2.1. Professional organizations have relationships with business partners and consultants, registered education providers (REPs), and educational institutions. Professional associations have relationships with all groups.

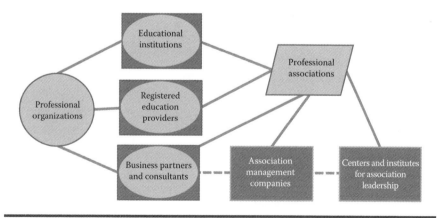

Figure 2.1   Interrelationships of professional associations and organizations.

Milestones in Professional Certification

In 1977, the National Commission for Health Certifying Agencies (NCHCA) was established to develop quality standards for voluntary professional certification programs. In 1989, the scope of those standards was increased to include professional certification across a multitude of occupations. The standard-setting and accrediting organization NCHCA became the National Commission for Certifying Agencies (NCCA), and the National Organization for Competency Assurance (NOCA) was formed as the membership association for credentialing bodies. For more than 30 years, NOCA, NCCA, and their predecessor promoted adherence to quality standards in professional certification. They currently promote best practices in credentialing through creating awareness, education, research, advocacy, setting standards, and accreditation.

As NOCA became the global leader in providing support to assist those pursuing professional certification, the board of directors noticed the need to restructure the organization. In 2009, NOCA became the Institute for Credentialing Excellence (ICE). Today, ICE is a nonprofit, 501(c)(3) organization focused on providing resources for the credentialing community and has more than 300 members. ICE's accrediting body, the NCCA, evaluates certification organization for compliance with the NCCA Standards for the Accreditation of professional certification programs. NCCA's standards exceed the requirements established by the American Psychological Association (APA) and U.S. Equal Employment Opportunity Commission (EEOC). ICE is accredited by the American National Standards Institute (ANSI) as a standards developer. Today, ICE is a professional membership association that provides information and supporting resources for professional associations and professional organizations and others who work in and serve the credentialing industry. ICE develops standards for professional certification and certificate programs) (CPs) and serves as a clearinghouse for professional certification and CPs.

Credentialing Authorities

Who certifies these programs to ensure they are professional and meet recommended standards? This is of great importance because a large percentage of certification programs are implemented by professional associations and professional organizations without the assistance of experienced certifying agencies. This may be due to a number of reasons, including but not limited to:

- The time it takes to follow recommended standards
- The complexity of adhering to guidelines for testing (psychometrics)
- Verified need for the certification
- Financial stability of institution proposing certification

- Marketplace demand for the certification
- Maturity of the certification being recognized as an occupation or profession

The frightening reality is that recipients of the certification are not aware of the issues surrounding what it takes for a professional certification to meet recommended standards. It is like going to a restaurant and eating food that has not been approved for human consumption. It might smell good at first and even have a nice taste. You might not even get sick, but if you do get sick, well, that is another story. Similarly, certification that does not follow recommended standards might leave a "bad taste in your mouth."

The most comprehensive book on national professional certification programs was published by HRD Press in conjunction with CRC Press (Barnhart, 1997). This was followed up a year later by a book that specifically discusses certifications for computer and network professionals (Christianson & Fajen, 1998). Previous to this period, little was published.

There are certification agencies at the local, state, and federal levels. professional certification is usually only an affirmation that the person has met specified requirements as outlined by the certification. Professional certification does not usually attest to the person's ability to perform the task. There are now an increasing number of these governing bodies that are becoming involved in the process of professional certification. Some of them certify and others support accreditation process, for example:

- The **Accrediting Commission of Career Schools and Colleges (ACCSC)** is listed by the U.S. Department of Education as a nationally recognized accrediting agency.
- The **Accrediting Council for Continuing Education and Training (ACCET)** has been officially recognized by the U.S. Department of Education since 1978 as a reliable authority regarding the quality of education and training provided by the institutions they accredit. In 1998, ACCET became the first accrediting agency to be certified as an International Organization for Standardization (ISO) 9001:2008 Quality Management System under the international standards established by ISO.
- The **Accreditation Board for Engineering and Technology (ABET)** is the accrediting agency for engineering, computing, technology, and applied science degree programs in the United States; it is composed of approximately 30 professional societies.
- The **American Council on Education Program on Non-collegiate Sponsored Instruction (ACE-PONSI)** is a designated team of content experts who are selected from ACE member college faculties; the team reviews courses and determines whether the training is comparable to college-level curriculum. If it is, ACE-PONSI recommends the appropriate number and level of credits that can be awarded for successful completion

of each course. ACE-PONSI's recommendations for college credits for non-academic organizations' courses create more opportunity for growth for professional certification.

- **ANSI** is comprised of companies, government agencies, organizations, academic and international bodies, and individuals. ANSI represents the interests of more than 125,000 companies and 3.5 million professionals. ANSI is actively engaged in accrediting programs that assess conformance to standards, including globally recognized cross-sector programs such as the ISO 9000 (quality) and ISO 14000 (environmental) management systems. ANSI oversees the development, promulgation, and use of thousands of standards and guidelines that have a direct impact on businesses in nearly every sector.
- The **Council on Accreditation (COA)** is an accrediting body for organizations that provide social and behavioral healthcare services to people in the United States and Canada.
- The **Certification Commission for Healthcare Interpreters (CCHI)** is the first organization to receive NCCA accreditation in the area of certifying healthcare interpreters. The commission supports nonprofit interpreting, language entities; community-based educational institutions; healthcare service providers; and the limited English proficient (LEP).
- The **Council of Engineering and Scientific Specialty Boards (CESB)** gives recognition only to the programs that have a full developed body of knowledge and utilize comprehensive examination and recertification processes. They take a deep look into the structure of the certification and its ability to operate and sustain itself.
- The **Defense Activity for Non-Traditional Education Support (DANTES)** supports the creation, direction, and management of education for veterans/service members and across the Department of Defense and education community to ensure quality and content validity.
- **ICE** is a professional membership association that provides education, networking, and other resources for organizations and individuals who work in and serve the credentialing industry.
- **Institute of Electrical and Electronics Engineers (IEEE)** professional certification programs were developed to help identify individuals who have the skills and knowledge deemed essential for professionals in a variety of fields.
- The **ISO** develops international standards but is not involved in the certification for any of the standards it develops. ISO certification is performed by external certification agencies. ISO's Committee on Conformity Assessment (CASCO) has produced standards that are based on international consensus on good certification practices. professional associations and professional organizations operate their professional certification activities in accordance with these international standards. When a professional certification from a professional associations and professional organizations is certified to an ISO standard, it receives a certificate from the certification body.

- The **NCCA** is the accrediting body of ICE, and its opinion is widely accepted as legitimate, independent verification that a certification program is statistically valid. To date, NCCA has accredited approximately 280 programs from more than 120 organizations. There are more than 100 organizations, representing over 250 programs, that have obtained and maintained NCCA accreditation in a wide range of professions. To be accredited, professional associations submit an application to NCCA to demonstrate that their professional certification programs are compliance with NCCA's Standards for the Accreditation of Certification Programs. Accreditation is usually valid for 5 years.
- The **National Center for Higher Education Management Systems (NCHEMS)** is an independent research firm that provides an external evaluation of the standards of accreditation and the commission's student achievement benchmarks. For example, in 2009, ACCSC contracted with NCHEMS to determine the degree that key constituents believed that the standards of accreditation were relevant to student learning and adequate for the purpose of assessing quality education.

Many regulatory agencies also have a vested interest in certification programs, especially those that are cross functional and improve competencies in information technology (IT), project management, quality, performance improvement, health and wellness, and so on. Let us take a look at some U.S. examples of how professional certification ties into their strategic vision, mission, and strategic imperatives:

- **Food and Drug Administration (FDA):** The FDA is responsible for protecting public health and welfare through the regulation and supervision of food, tobacco, drug products, medical devices, and the like. The FDA has a vested interested in those professional certification that focus on the pharmaceutical industry, for instance, the Certified Pharmaceutical Industry Professional (CPIP) offered by the International Society of Pharmaceutical Engineering (ISPE).
- **Federal Emergency Management Agency (FEMA):** FEMA coordinates the response to a disaster that has occurred in the United States that cannot be effectively addressed by local and state authorities. FEMA has a vested interest in those professional certification that focus on disaster recovery; for instance, the American Board for Certification in Homeland Security (CHS®) sponsors the Certified in Disaster Preparedness (CDP-I®) certification program.
- **Occupational Safety and Health Administration (OSHA):** OSHA is the main federal agency charged with the enforcement of safety and health legislation. OSHA focuses on four strategies: (1) leadership; (2) strong, fair, and effective enforcement; (3) outreach, education, and compliance assistance; and (4) partnerships. OSHA has a stake in the Certified Safety Professional (CSP) offered by the Board of Certified Safety Professionals (BCSP).

- **Environmental Protection Agency (EPA):** The EPA was created for the purpose of safeguarding human health and the environment by writing and enforcing regulations. The agency has a "go green" stake in the Certified Environmental Professional (CEP) offered by the National Association of Environmental Professionals (NAEP).

Centers and Institutes for Association Leadership

The long-term success of a professional association depends on the centers and institutes for association leadership. This is due to the enormous, but situation-specific, requirements to support professional associations on an ongoing basis. In one respect, these entities can be thought of as an association for AMCs. Examples in the United States include the Association Management Companies Institute (AMCI) and American Society of Association Executives (ASAE).

The AMCI has more than 165 member companies and provides turnkey service management to more than 1,750 clients and specific project work to more than 860 groups. This number represents more than 3,800 staff managed by AMC members. AMCI was formerly the International Association of Association Management Companies (IAAMC), a nonprofit international trade association with more than 150 AMC members throughout the United States, Canada, Europe, and Asia.

The ASAE works closely with AMCI to support strategic imperatives and budgets of these clients, which collectively represents more than $1 billion managed by these AMC members. The ASAE represents more than 21,000 association executives and industry partners representing 10,000 organizations. ASAE is headquartered in Washington, D.C., and AMCI is in close proximity in Alexandria, Virginia.

On May 21, 2007, AMCI and ASAE joined forces on their accreditation program. There is now a single industry accreditation supported by associations and AMCs. This was necessary to provide clearer direction to associations interested in being managed by AMCs. The AMCI and ASAE (the Center for Association Leadership) have agreed to come together to fully support a single AMC accreditation program.

Each of these organizations (AMCI and ASAE) performs slightly different functions, which can be seen by reviewing their individual websites (respectively http://www.amcinstitute.org/ and http://www.asaecenter.org/).

They collectively have a huge charter:

- Educate AMCs so they can support professional associations and professional organizations
- Maintain representation from a large segment of the professional associations and professional organizations population
- Serve as a conduit to enable association leadership to express concerns
- Advocate with political officials to lobby for associations at the highest levels

- Offer certification to association executives (i.e., Certified Association Executive, CAE)
- Coordinate accreditation
- Collaborate with the global marketplace to support international association objectives
- Enable private social networking opportunities to support best practices
- Incorporate education programs in a virtual university setting
- Address laws and regulations and provide connections to legal services
- Establish the ethical frameworks by which professional associations and professional organizations should operate
- Help determine compensation guidelines for association staff members
- Outline competencies for association staff members
- Host job search agents for job seekers and employers
- Research and provide business intelligence to aid in decision making
- Facilitate national and local conferences to bring together association leaders
- Publish trade journals or magazines to represent industry concerns

Association Management Companies

An AMC provides specialized services to professional associations using a for-profit approach that runs a nonprofit/not-for-profit association like a business. It provides expert advice to professional associations. Professional organizations do not typically utilize the service of an AMC because they are already businesses with this expertise. Why are AMCs important? A professional association has to make a determination if it will hire internal staff to perform operational functions or if it will outsource these tasks. AMCs can provide professional associations and professional organizations with support staff to carry out business functions. Many professional associations and professional organizations are challenged with fluctuating demands for services and may utilize AMCs periodically to perform the following activities:

- Coordination with business partners and consultants
- Website development and management services
- Administrative support and accounting (receivables and collection)
- Customer service and materials fulfillment
- Membership database management
- Public relations, sales, and marketing support
- IT (cloud computing)
- Event planning for annual conferences and speaker coordination
- Newsletter and trade journal publishing
- Board member professional development
- Certification exam preparation (psychometrics)
- Certification course material development

- Financial reinvestment advice
- Succession planning and business continuity planning

A random Internet search in January 2013 revealed a number of companies that offer association management services. These include partial service (specialized) and full service. Many of these companies will reference ASAE or AMCI on their website. They may also draw special attention if they are an ANSI standards developer. (*Note:* Listing of these companies is not intended to be an endorsement of their services.) Examples of AMCs include:

- **Agentis (full service):** Provides support in publication services, government affairs, fundraising, social media, and project management.
- **Kellen Company (full service):** A professional services company that offers management, public relations, web development, meetings, marketing, and consulting services. The company serves a diversified client base on an international basis.
- **Knapp International (partial service/specialized):** A consulting firm specializing in the development and revitalization of professional certification programs. Since 1989, they have been involved in strategic thinking, change management, new product development and implementation, psychometrics, and new program evaluation.
- **Professional Management Associates (PMA) (full-service):** An AMC that provides association management services to trade associations, professional societies, nonprofit organizations, business networks, user groups, membership organizations, and donor-supported foundations.
- **SmithBucklin (full service):** Provides management and outsourcing services to 320 trade associations, professional societies, technology user groups, corporations, and government institutes/agencies. These services include convention and event management, exhibit and trade show management, marketing and communications, web and technology management, and education programs.

Business Partners and Consultants

Business partners and consultants are third-party solution providers (i.e., vendors) who provide products or services (i.e., exam preparation materials, conference support, etc.) in support of professional associations and professional organizations certification programs. Comparatively speaking, they are more limited in scope when compared to an AMC. The products and services they provide are competitively priced and of acceptable quality. There should be some evaluation system put in place to qualify vendors who will provide products and services so certificants know what is best to purchase.

Some companies, because of how they are set up, may not be in a position to become a REP due to a number of circumstances, such as:

- Fees associated with being a REP (i.e., can run into the thousands per year)
- Noncompete clauses if offering product or service to a competing professional association
- Similarity of product or service when compared to an existing REP
- Volume of potential revenue

Therefore, as resources are identified to support professional certification, other supporting solution providers should be considered in addition to REPs. Some resources provided by other providers are available free of charge (i.e., sample test questions) and address specific requirements for achieving or maintaining professional certification. In some cases, identifying these other service providers can be done by:

- looking in the professional association's online bookstore
- searching the consultant directory
- reviewing articles or advertisements in the professional association's trade journal
- conducting a focused wild-card Internet search

There are thousands of companies that have become connected with professional associations and professional organizations to offer products and services in support of certification. Many of these businesses provide career opportunities for certificants. Some examples of business partners and consultants include:

- **Advisicon:** Solutions provider in the IT arena that configures Microsoft product offerings (i.e., Project Server and SharePoint) and delivers training courses through Advisicon University.
- **AXA Equitable:** Member retirement planning for professional association staff.
- **Applied Measurement Professionals (AMP):** Provides certification organizations, government agencies, professional associations, and private industry with psychometric consultation, testing, measurement, and management solutions.
- **BoardnetUSA.org:** A networking website that helps professional associations and prospective board members find each other.
- **BoardSource.org:** Publishes a series of documents to support the board of directors (BOD).
- **Certificationstation.org:** Designs, develops, and delivers customized courses (i.e., e-learning, instructor guides, participant materials, etc.) for professional associations and professional organizations.
- **Data Sense Solutions:** Provides training on business objects and data warehousing.

■ **Documation:** A full-service provider of print and related services to organizations. This program provides a printing royalty, based on sales volume, to the professional associations and professional organizations.

■ **Exit Certified:** IT training company that offers certification for vendors such as SAP, IBM, Red Hat, Oracle, Symantec, Apple, Hitachi, and MySQL.

■ **Holmes Corporation:** Works with associations to create, market, and distribute certification exam preparation products globally. It is involved in instructional design, marketing, and channel management/distribution.

■ **International Institute for Learning (IIL):** A global leader in training, consulting, coaching, and customized course development with a presence in more than 200 countries. IIL's core competencies include project, program, and portfolio management; business analysis; Microsoft° Project and Project Server; Lean Six Sigma; PRINCE2°; ITIL°; Agile; leadership and interpersonal skills; corporate consciousness; and sustainability. IIL is a registered education partner of PMI and a Microsoft Gold Partner, among other strategic relationships.

■ **Knapp International (specialized service):** A consulting firm specializing in the development and revitalization of professional certification programs. Since 1989, they have been involved in strategic thinking, change management, new product development and implementation, psychometrics, and new program evaluation.

■ **Marsh:** Offers insurance programs, including association professional liability.

■ **Professional Convention Management Association (PCMA):** PCMA represents more than 6,000 meeting industry leaders internationally. PCMA has 17 chapters in the United States, Canada, and Mexico; membership includes planner and trade show/exhibit professionals, suppliers, faculty, students, and emeriti.

■ **Prometric:** A wholly owned subsidiary of Educational Testing Service (ETS) and a trusted provider of technology-enabled testing and assessment solutions.

■ **Pearson:** Provides expertise across a wide range of educational and testing, including item and test development, scoring and reporting, and research and analysis.

■ **True Solutions:** A career school and college approved by the Texas Workforce Commission. It offers programs targeting skill improvement and competency development.

■ **Webster, Chamberlain & Bean:** Legal consultation services.

Professional Association versus Professional Organization

What is the difference between a professional certification offered by a professional association compared to that offered by an organization (i.e., technology solutions provider) (Table 2.1)? In other words, what is the difference between professional certification offered by an organization, such as the International Information Systems Security Certification Consortium (ISC)², compared to that offered by Cisco, for instance?

The person pursing the professional certification may not see any noticeable difference in a professional certification offered by a professional association compared to a professional organization. In the example, the assumption is that both the professional association and professional organization:

- Have a good industry reputation
- Maintain adequate staff to support certification
- Embrace continuous improvement
- Offer professional certification that are in demand
- Deliver comprehensive support for their professional certification programs
- Make certification preparation materials available
- Require certificants to follow a code of conduct

Table 2.1 Comparison of a Professional Association to a Professional Organization

Item	Professional Association	Professional Organization
Membership	Usually offered	Not usually offered
Focus	Developing member competencies	Supporting a product or service with more knowledgeable resources
Target areas	Body of knowledge	Hands-on experience
Support for study groups	Free of charge or at minimal cost	Varies and limited access
Supporting conferences	Lots of availability	Limited to moderate availability by comparison
Industry demand	Low to high	Moderate to high by comparison due to its association with a product or service
Revenue growth	Nonprofit/not for profit	For profit

It is somewhat unfortunate that while many professional organizations have done an outstanding job implementing professional certification programs, they are not usually positioned to provide similar ongoing member benefits to certificants when compared to a professional association. This may be in part due to:

- Professional organizations are for-profit companies, whereas professional associations are usually nonprofit or not for profit.
- Professional organizations develop separate channels for communications and networking under the umbrella of no-profits, which are independent and outside their business and certification programs. This makes good sense for legal reasons. For example, the International Association of Microsoft Channel Partners (IAMCP), established in 1994 has a voice in Microsoft and the IT community at large. It facilitates growth and business development among partners.
- Confusion might result for a company like Microsoft to have dual representation as a company and an association.
- It might not be profitable for a professional organization to start chapters in medium-large metropolitan cities.

Some of the differences (viewed as benefits) in the "service" associated with the professional certification offered by the professional association pertains to ongoing support that comes through the professional association in the form of:

- Networking (i.e., at local chapter meetings)
- Access to larger forums (i.e., national/global conferences)
- Publications (i.e., trade journals)
- Information exchange (i.e., website presence)
- Ongoing courses, webinars, and conferences to support certification maintenance
- Professional association BOD (i.e., to provide a point of contact) (i.e., not sales oriented)
- Opportunities for volunteering

Professional Association Governance and Membership

Professional association governance involves the processes by which a professional association functions and sustains itself. These activities include:

- Accounting and finance
- Tracking and communicating with membership
- Reserving facilities and ordering refreshments
- Coordinating meetings and speakers
- Networking for best practices
- Handling job leads and referrals

■ Supporting job analysis and competency development
■ Raising funds and collecting donations

Other important functions that best-in-class professional associations also offer include:

■ Coordinating tours at local companies to promote best practices
■ Engaging senior leadership from various companies to attend chapter meetings and make presentations
■ Creating rewards and recognition programs for individual members (i.e., outstanding volunteers) and companies (i.e., company of the year)
■ Offering ongoing study groups and forums that will allow additional opportunity to earn PDUs (professional development units) or CEUs (continuing education units)
■ Attracting good speakers to deliver up-to-date relevant content that will increase the number of attendees at chapter meetings and events

It is usually the responsibility of the local BOD to identify volunteers who will help perform the tasks listed. The local BOD follows prescribed bylaws and is supported by the national association to provide management and leadership of the professional association at the chapter level. The revised chapter bylaws are proposed to the Chapter membership for the upcoming election of new officers and if accepted will be formally effective the next operating year. The following is an outline of bylaws that are common to a professional association:

■ Bylaw I: Name; principal office; other offices
■ Bylaw II: Relationship to the professional association
■ Bylaw III: Purpose and limitations of the chapter
■ Bylaw IV: Chapter membership
■ Bylaw V: Chapter governance and operations
■ Bylaw VI: Chapter nominations and elections
■ Bylaw VII: Chapter committees
■ Bylaw VIII: Chapter finance
■ Bylaw IX: Meetings of the membership
■ Bylaw X: Inurement and conflict of interest
■ Bylaw XI: Indemnification
■ Bylaw XII: Adoption and amendments
■ Bylaw XIII: Dissolution

Note: If you are going to be affiliated with a professional association and a member of the local chapter, it is important to become familiar with the bylaws. It takes less than an hour to review them.

The local BOD should ensure the professional association is welcoming and supportive to its membership.

The local chapter should support professional development, professional certification, and networking activities. While the chapter meets current member needs, it sometimes becomes necessary to communicate with the national professional association office. Professional association national offices should welcome member visits and communication. It is important for the local BOD and members to maintain a close relationship with the national association. There are several venues that may offer this opportunity, such as national conferences, global webcasts, or site visits to the national headquarters.

The local chapter professional association BOD typically has these roles:

- President: Responsible for overall chapter leadership
- Past president: Serves in a transitional role to support overall governance
- Vice president of marketing: Promotes chapter services to generate revenues
- Vice president of administration/operations: Logistics and coordination
- Vice president of programs: Selects speakers
- Vice president of education: Coordinates study groups and educational activities
- Vice president of membership: Plans chapter growth
- Vice president of finance: Oversees chapter revenues
- Vice president of outreach: Collaborates with other organizations
- Director of volunteers: Promotes volunteering
- Director or sponsorship: Encourages donations
- Director of mentorship/coaching: Supports member professional development
- Legal counsel
- Secretary

Regarding professional association membership, an important consideration for choosing to be a member of a professional association is not only the professional certification but also the benefits given to the member. This being said, if a person is going to pursue a professional certification from a professional association, then it makes sense to join the professional association to establish a firm relationship with it. Some of the benefits of professional association membership include:

- Networking with other professionals and special interest groups
- Access to information regarding your field of interest
- Publications (in some cases there may be choices)
- Discounts on chapter meetings and national conferences
- Discounts on certification exam fee and preparation materials
- Webinars and online meetings
- Job search listings and ability to reference professional association on your résumé
- Fun that comes along with joining a professional association

Joining a professional association should be taken seriously because it requires a financial and time investment. Moreover, when you join a professional association, it reflects on you, especially if you hold a professional certification issued by the professional association. Therefore, research should go into the selection process before making a decision. Here are some things to consider as you conduct research on the professional association:

■ How long has the professional association been established?
■ Where is the member base (i.e., national or international)?
■ What is the financial stability of the professional association? professional associations are usually nonprofit or not for profit. However, they can generate large revenues and provide many services to members.
■ Who is providing customer service, and does the experience feel welcoming?
■ When is the professional association available for communication and by what means (i.e., telephone)?

Due to the economics associated with maintaining office space, especially in larger cities, some professional associations may work virtually. In other words, they may have a website, mailing address, and phone number but limited or no physical offices. Considering that many dues for professional associations are approaching $125 to $200 per year and more, it is always worth questioning the level and quality of communication you are receiving. I have personally been more impressed with the many site visits I have conducted where the professional association has staff members that you can meet personally and have your questions answered. If a professional association fails to provide this opportunity, it may be necessary to ask why before making time and financial investments. Usually, when you become involved with a professional association, it turns into a multiple-year commitment, longer if you obtain the professional certification.

Another way to get and stay connected with the professional association is by utilizing social media, such as Facebook, Twitter, and LinkedIn. When networking, ask those certified these questions:

■ Why did you become a member of this professional association?
■ When did you join this professional association?
■ Would you recommend other people to join this professional association?
■ Where else did you look before joining this professional association?
■ Who is a board member at a local chapter so I can speak with a local member?
■ What is the process for certification?

The first year of membership is a good time to get to know the members by attending chapter meetings and conferences. It is also beneficial to review the articles and trade journals. The second year of membership is a good time to get involved as a volunteer.

Professional Organization Structure and Community Members

Many professional organizations who have certification offerings are corporations in the IT industry, such as Apple, Cisco, Hewlett-Packard, Microsoft, Novell, and Oracle. The focus of these certifications is hardware (i.e., computers), networks and peripherals, or software (i.e., Windows, Linux, or Java). It is complimentary and fair to refer to the companies listed as giants.

The organizational structure of a giant professional organization is usually functional. It may seem difficult to navigate some of these structures. Functional organizational structures are set up by department. Professional organization structure as it pertains to supporting professional certification may consist of these functions:

- Research and development
- Sales and marketing
- Public relations
- Vendor management
- Operations
- Human resources
- Information technology
- Training (instruction design and curriculum development)
- Customer service
- Membership management (certificant relations)
- Fulfillment (i.e., production, printing, and assembly)
- Quality assurance/quality control
- Logistics: supply chain management (i.e., shipping, inventory, warehouse management)
- Finance and accounting
- Legal

Regarding professional organization community members, professional organizations commonly refer to those who have become certified members of the community (online), subscribers, or certificants. This is because there is usually no direct association membership (i.e., in Microsoft for those who obtain MCSE (Microsoft Certified Systems Engineer) or other types of Microsoft certification). While there is no direct membership, certificants still may seek to affiliate themselves with these companies. This makes sense for these reasons:

- Membership has its benefits and so does networking with other professionals who have achieved the certification.
- The professional organization has a good industry reputation, such as Red Hat or VMWare. By connecting the certification to the professional organization, there is instant acknowledgment of the certification value.

- The professional organization offers a road map to support ongoing professional development. For example, HP ExpertOne issues career certifications for levels from associate to master.
- The cross-platform and independent nature of some certifications (i.e., Linux is not owned by any company as it is an open source application). Those people who become certified in Linux might desire a training affiliation with Novell, which offers a Certified Linux Professional (CLP) certification.
- There are discounts for those who are connected to the certification.
- It holds the professional organization accountable to maintain the certification and keep it up to date.

As a result of the huge economic opportunity that professional certification represents, it is important that due diligence is performed on an ongoing basis to ensure that the individual who has the professional certification realizes the most from that investment.

Registered Education Providers

Vendors (and sometimes employers) who meet the qualifications for educational content delivery as specified by the professional associations and professional organizations can become classified as a Registered Education Provider (REP). A REP can be critical to the success of a professional associations and professional organizations and professional certification by providing

- books (i.e., on related topics) and publications (i.e., trade journals)
- online training (i.e., e-learning) and on-site training (i.e., instructor-led workshops)
- conferences (i.e., to address specific content in greater detail)
- exam preparation materials (i.e., database of sample questions)
- supplementary support services (i.e., IT such as a Learning Management System (LMS)

There are many potential benefits of using a REP:

- It balances the staff requirements of a professional association by enabling certain functions to be handled by the REP and thereby provides member value by increasing response time.
- A working relationship has been established between the REP and professional association.
- The quality of materials produced has been reviewed or approved.
- It controls the number and type of vendors producing certification-related materials.
- The REP's registered courses are established in the professional association's system, allowing for a transcript to be generated for the student that lists PDUs or CEUs completed.

- It enables the professional association to charge a fee for REP status, thereby increasing revenue to the professional association.

Note: Some businesses are able to establish themselves as a REP. They can then train their own employees and invite other companies to participate in the delivery of their professional certification courses.

Educational Institutions

An educational institution is a postsecondary school that is capable of providing a learning environment conducive for adults. Technical colleges and community colleges (TC&CC) generally appear to have an environment that works well for professional associations and professional organizations. If the school has a multiuse facility philosophy, it can be especially attractive to professional associations that need to hold monthly chapter meetings and coordinate study groups. If the professional certification is offered through TC&CC, then other academic discounts may be available to the professional association. TC&CC can also serve as good venues to hold chapter board meetings and events. When board meetings are held, a conference room may be the preferred option. Events such as certification recognition or social networking can work well in TC&CC.

Many TC&CC have part-time or adjunct instructors who welcome the opportunity to collaborate with a professional association to deliver professional certification courses. This can result in high-quality delivery at an affordable price usually if there is a long-term agreement in place. TC&CC may also be willing to rent the use of their facilities for a reasonable cost (i.e., offices, copiers, computers, and office phones during off-peak hours, which is typically when professional associations and professional organizations hold meetings and events). The appropriate protocol is always to seek permission to ensure relationships remain good.

The only concern that naturally arises is to ensure that other students and faculty respect the course delivery and do not interrupt the sessions in progress by asking questions, sitting in to observe, and so on. Because professional certification may involve professionals of all ages and TC&CC may represent a younger crowd by comparison, it is also important that the group is comfortable with the environment visited.

Employers

The employer has a stake in helping the employee obtain certification. Some employers are willing to support this investment in human capital, and others are trying to determine if professional credential is really worth it in the end. Therefore, it is important to ask:

- How does professional credential affect the bottom line?
- How does it have an impact on a person's pay?
- What is the incentive for the employer?
- What role does the employer play in the certification process?

From the employer's perspective, people should be compensated correctly. According to Fine and Getkate (1995), there are primarily two ways to pay people fairly and equitably:

1. Based on complexity in comparison to other jobs.
2. Based on their personal skills; the more skills (i.e., certifications) they bring to the job, the more they will be worth.

In many cases, the employer may be requested to support professional credential. This is because:

- Certification costs may be requested by the employee to help pay for certification exams, study materials, or travel.
- The nature of the professional credential content is complex (i.e., IT related). Vendors may find the material difficult to develop without the assistance of the employer.
- There is a need to utilize facilities and resources the employer can make available (i.e., meeting rooms to facilitate study groups or copiers to reproduce materials).
- Verification of work products may require the employer to confirm projects.

Critics

Why do some people criticize certification? Is everyone who is involved in certification doing the right thing? Are all certifications professional? ANSI, in Standard 1100, specifies the requirements for meeting the ANSI standard for a certifying organization. According to this standard, a professional certifying organization must:

1. Deliver an assessment based on the industry body of knowledge (BOK), independent from training courses or course providers
2. Grant a time-limited credential to anyone who meets the assessment standards

The flowchart in Figure 2.2 illustrates the process that can be followed to avoid criticism.

Not only does ANSI have these standards, but also other agencies (i.e., NCCA) involved in accreditation similarly have requirements that must be followed. professional certification providers who do not meet the criteria specified by accrediting

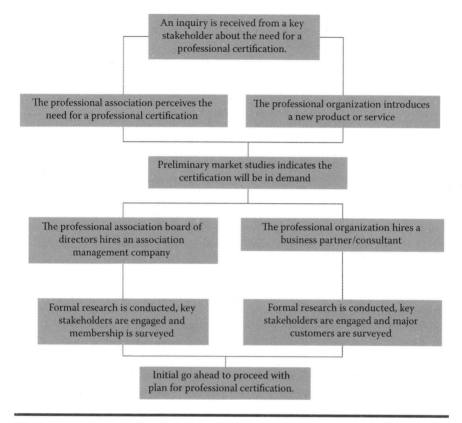

Figure 2.2   Initial process flow for new professional certification programs.

agencies become subject to criticism. For example, it is reported that more than 10% of certifications have no eligibility requirements (Knapp and Associates, 2007). Other reasons why people speak negatively about certification include the following:

1. They see some professional associations and professional organizations as not professional, lacking adherence to good practices.
2. They notice abuse of the certification (i.e., a person making false claims).
3. They see people pursuing certifications undergoing stress, hardship, or other difficulties and determine that the investment is a sacrifice not worth making.
4. They hear about the horror stories from degree mills that cheat people into pursuing seemingly worthless certifications.
5. They may not currently prefer virtual social networking or in-person networking that is normally customary for people who achieve professional certification.

6. They are disgruntled at the level of effort and investment required to maintain professional certification.
7. They do not want to make the financial investment.
8. They may perceive large revenues being generated by a professional associations and professional organizations and do not understand where the money goes to support professional certification, raising concern.

When is enough not enough and too many too much? Have you ever been really full of food, but unsatisfied and still wanting something else? Some people might find reasons to complain when there is no legitimate reason. For example, there are some professional associations that offer only one professional certification. Other professional associations may offer multiple professional certification. For example, as of 2013, the American Society for Quality (ASQ) offered 17 certifications. So, it really is not important how many professional certification are offered, but rather that the quality of the professional certification is good.

Suggested Reading

Christianson, J., and Fajen, A. (1998). *Computer and Network Professional Certification Guide*. Alameda, CA: Sybex.

Fine, S., and Getkate, M. (1995). *Benchmark Tasks for Job Analysis: A Guide for Functional Job Analysis (FJA) Scales*. Mahwah, NJ: Erlbaum.

Knapp and Associates International. (2007). Knapp Certification Industry Scan. Princeton, NJ: Knapp International.

Knapp, L., and Gallery, M. (2003). *Credentialing Essentials: What to Consider Before Starting a Certification Program*. Association Management, November. Washington, DC: American Society of Association Executives.

Chapter 3

Preparing for Professional Certification

Key Lessons

- Getting Answers to Frequently Asked Questions
- Mastering the Body of Knowledge
- Financing Professional Certification
- Accessing the Professional Certification Handbook
- Filling Out the Professional Association Membership Application
- Interpreting the Professional Certification Application
- Previewing the Different Types of Certification Fees and Dues
- Clarifying the Types of Professional Certification Assessments
- Optimizing Certification Preparation Resources
- Determining Test-Taking Strategies
- Overcoming Anxiety and Mental Blocks
- Completing the Readiness Assessment

Getting Answers to Frequently Asked Questions

Those who are pursuing certification from professional associations and professional organizations should create a laundry list of questions and search diligently on the Internet to answer them:

- What are my real interests regarding a career and certification?

- How do my knowledge, skills, and abilities align with a prospective certification path?
- What are the affordable certification paths, considering time, cost, and energy?
- Where should I obtain certification?
- How much is the certification worth in terms of marketplace demand?
- What can be done to maximize my investment in the certification?
- Which certifications should be selected?
- Where should I access certification material?
- When should I get started?
- Who can help me if I have more questions?
- If I do not become certified, how will it have an impact on my long-term career objectives?

Mastering the Body of Knowledge

A body of knowledge (BOK) represents the concepts, ideas, language, and terminology associated with a professional domain. A BOK may include a functional job description that addresses the roles and responsibilities of people engaged in that line of work. Professional domains are generic for the most part and attempt to capture practitioners' knowledge from different industries and occupations, such as:

- Training and development (T&D)
- Project management (PM)
- Human resource (HR) management
- Supply chain management (SCM)
- Legal
- Information technology (IT)
- Healthcare
- Hospitality

Some professional domains focus on general industry understanding, and others are specialized. When specialized, there can be more than one BOK. While both professional associations and professional organizations utilize BOKs, professional associations are frequently established specifically to support professional domains. For example, a professional association may invite those involved in HR to its chapter meetings regardless of the industry, provided their job role is in HR. Conversely, a professional organization may only invite those to a learning event who have a specific interest in a software application. A professional domain is operationally defined by groups such as industry, government, education, and professional associations and professional organizations. Professional domains are affected by factors such as the country, location, and culture.

Most professional domains have a BOK. However, not every BOK is currently published in the same format. This may be due to a number of reasons:

- Focus of the BOK: Some are focused on exam certification, others on job type.
- Obtaining input from industry.
- Support of a related professional association.
- Reaching voluntary consensus.
- Cost of publication and keeping it current.

For identification purposes, a prefix frequently precedes the BOK. For example, the *Project Management Body of Knowledge PMBOK Guide*, 5th edition represents a project management knowledge framework published by the Project Management Institute (PMI). The *PMBOK Guide* describes the sum of knowledge within the project management profession. The *PMBOK Guide* was created in 1983 and has been revised several times since then; currently, it is in its fifth edition, published January 2013. A BOK is usually developed by a professional associations and professional organizations with input from its membership or subject matter experts (SMEs). The BOK is important for a number of reasons:

- Represents agreed-on knowledge for a discipline or occupation
- Establishes operational definitions for a professional domain
- Promotes a common language for professional associations and professional organizations
- Outlines inputs, outputs, tools, and techniques associated with processes
- Provides a framework by which tasks are carried out
- Incorporates standards, which are related guidelines for topic areas

Note: Standards are developed through member consensus and may be separate documents.

Financing Professional Certification

How are you intending to pay for the professional certification? Take a look at the potential investment:

- Professional certification application (PCA)
- Professional association membership dues
- Professional certification study course
- Professional certification study materials (i.e., books, exam simulations software, flash cards)
- Travel costs to attend related conferences and earn professional development units (PDUs)

- Travel costs to attend study groups
- Ongoing courses to maintain professional certification

Here are some of the options worth considering:

- For individuals who have experienced corporate downsizing, there may be a provision for retraining funds. This frequently covers the cost of professional certification. Generous provisions are made by companies in support of this initiative.
- Scholarships are available to those who qualify. These are typically needs based.
- Tuition reimbursement is usually available. However, preapproval is required in many instances to justify the expenditures.
- Expense reimbursement may be the option where tuition reimbursement makes the process overly complex and the company has determined that the professional certification is valuable.
- Joining the professional association usually presents opportunities for discounts or more opportunities to network and obtain professional certification resources (i.e., through a shared library arrangement).
- Educational loans may be available through the bank or credit union, which may be less expensive than putting costs on a credit card.

Accessing the *Professional Certification Handbook*

The purpose of the professional certification handbook (PCH) is to provide a comprehensive description of the professional certification. It prepares the person for the professional certification and serves multiple purposes:

- It emphasizes the benefits of the certification through marketplace analysis.
- It outlines the different types of exams and requirements.
- It provides key contact information on how to apply for the certification.
- It lists criteria for applying for professional certification (i.e., work experience, education, assessment scores).
- It discusses the process for obtaining (i.e., including timeframes for exam results) and maintaining the certification (i.e., PDUs per year).
- It details the costs for the certification application and assessment (i.e., exam).
- It describes the costs and process for retaking the exam (if applicable).
- It covers job analysis (i.e., role delineation study) information.
- It indicates which tasks and activities are performed by the individual.
- It outlines which competencies are desired.
- It outlines which skills and abilities are required.
- It outlines what knowledge is required.

Other essential topics that may also be covered in the PCH include:

- Preparing for the exam and test-taking tips
- Chapter/study group support information
- Available exam preparation material
- Industry/discipline BOK that is used as a foundation
- General description of code of ethics and professional conduct

Filling Out the Professional Association Membership Application

As noted, professional organizations do not typically offer membership for their professional certification because they are companies that offer professional certification as it relates to their products or services. So, the information that follows applies primarily to professional associations. Most of the information on a professional association membership application is straightforward. However, some of these items may require attention:

- Membership start date and expiration date: Most professional associations use a 1-year period for the start and expiration dates for membership. However, other professional associations work on a calendar year basis, and a membership begins on January 1 and expires on December 31 of the year. Professional associations that follow this arrangement and begin memberships on January 1 may or may not prorate fees.
- Membership directory listing: This is beneficial for networking purposes. It might be worth inquiring what contact information is available to those who have obtained professional certification previously so the interested professional certification applicant can have his or her questions answered.
- Individual discounts: Periodically, savings will be available during conferences or at the end of the year if the professional association is having a membership drive.
- Group rates: Corporate rates can result in substantial savings, especially if everyone does not need a printed journal and can access information electronically.
- Supplementary costs: Some items may be included, others available at an additional cost: publications, special interest groups, and local chapter affiliation.
- Illegal tying agreements: It is permissible for a professional associations and professional organizations to offer discounts to members or prospects to give incentive for them to join the organization or participate in certain groups to receive a discount on the professional certification exam or related products and services. This is considered creative marketing. However, they should not be forced to join the professional association.

Interpreting the Professional Certification Application

There are primarily four components of the PCA that represent a profile:

- Candidate education
  - Many professional associations look for a minimum of a bachelor's degree. Some professional associations look more closely at a related bachelor's degree. If a bachelor's degree has not been earned, then more hours of experience may be required to apply for professional certification.
- Candidate employment
  - Sometimes, it is necessary to look at work experience as a series of projects and to create a résumé that is focused on project accomplishments.
  - There should be little, if any, breaks (or gaps) in employment history. If appropriate, note any project engagements during transitional periods.
- Candidate's experience
  - Employment experience should relate to core competencies (behavioral as well as technical).
- Candidate's contact information
  - The use of a mailing address may be the best long-term solution.
- Certification examination
  - Certification-related course completion (i.e., PDUs) should be included.
  - Retain course certificates because these are vital records.

Note: Some professional associations offer the capability of an online transcript, which enables the professional association member (PAM) to record and track the courses he or she has taken.

Completing the PCA requires attention to detail. Failure to complete it properly results in:

- Possible audit
- Rejection of the application
- Delay of processing the PCH
- Recording incorrect information (i.e., address or name)

Why do some people have problems completing a PCA correctly?

- The application is foreign and not in their native language.
- Terms in the PCA use jargon or have seemingly more than one meaning.
- The person is confused about how to respond, so the person responds as he or she feels appropriate.
- They feel the need to stretch their experience as much as possible so they do not experience rejection in their application.

Some professional certification applicants experience concern as they attempt to get their application approved. This is not necessarily the result of a failure to complete the application correctly but of requirements that some professional associations and professional organizations have to systematically audit "X" number of applications. The primary purpose of an audit is to ensure that due diligence exists in the PCA. When completing the PCA,

- Market your experience using strong verbs as descriptors whenever possible: use *facilitated* instead of *participated in, directed* instead of *coordinated,* and so on.
- Utilize the framework recommended by the *PMBOK Guide* to list projects based on process groups (initiating, planning, executing, monitoring/controlling, and closing) or knowledge areas (communications, cost, HR, integration, procurement, quality, risk, scope, stakeholder, and time).

It is important to carefully read the policies and procedures related to the professional certification to avoid any embarrassment pertaining to a lack of clarification. Failure to follow directions on a PCA can cause a delay or may result in a future audit of paperwork. To ensure seamless collection of paperwork, it is helpful to create a checklist with four column headings (Table 3.1).

Completing the professional certification electronically, if available, is a preferred option. Before submitting the PCA, make a copy and file it. Make note of the date mailed, faxed, or e-mailed.

Table 3.1 Professional Certification Required Paperwork Checklist

Date Required	Item Required	Description	Check If Complete
1/1/2014	Projects	List of projects completed: start date, finish date	✓
2/1/2014	Transcripts	Bachelor's and master's degree must be certified	✓
3/1/2014	Résumé	CV Preferred	✓
5/1/2015	References	3 Professional	✓
6/1/2015	Application	Faxed	✓
7/1/2015	PDUs/CEUs	Verifiable	✓
8/1/2015	Other	Portfolio	✓

Regarding test administration, some PCAs will request that you specify how you would like the test delivered. For example, you may have a choice between paper and pencil or computer based. It is preferable to select computer based because results will usually come sooner. It may also give you options for what testing center you would like to attend. It is always important to select the testing center location that is most convenient to the test taker. You may receive an inquiry to go to another test center if a choice begins to fill. If you feel strongly about a test center location, then you should make it known to the professional associations and professional organizations or testing center if contact information has been made available to confirm your attendance there.

Previewing the Different Types of Certification Fees and Dues

The fees charged for a professional certification will vary depending on the circumstances:

- Certification application fee (member and nonmember)
- Certification renewal fee (member and nonmember)
- Certification renewal late fee (member and nonmember)
- Certification exam fee (member and nonmember)
- Retake certification exam fee due exam failure (member and nonmember)
- Lifetime member certification fee
- Certification transmittal fee
- Portfolio/work product review fee
- Certificate printing and mounting fee
- Duplicate certificate/replacement fee
- Examination rescheduling fee
- Examination score report fee
- Duplicate score report fee
- Certification reinstatement fee if expired
- Certification transcript fee for PDUs/CEUs (continuing education units)
- Annual association membership dues (national association)
- Annual association membership dues (local association)
- Chapter meeting dinner fee
- Annual conference fee
- Special interest group dues
- Cancellation of certification exam fee

Clarifying the Type
of Professional Certification Assessments

As mentioned in the first chapter, there are actually 10 possible meanings of the word *assessment*:

1. Education
2. Work history
3. Presentation of related work products (portfolio)
4. Test (multiple choice, true/false, yes/no, choose all that apply, drag and drop, matching, etc.)
5. Documented study hours, intended to confirm exam preparation
6. Demonstrated ability to perform the task
7. Personality, attitude, and behavior analysis (emotional intelligence)
8. Written examination (essay)
9. Oral examination (this can be performed through a panel of experts)
10. Quizzes using other senses (hearing, feeling, smelling, tasting, seeing)

It is important to note that not every professional associations and professional organizations requires the successful passing of an exam (i.e., multiple-choice test through a certified testing center) for its professional certification. It is also important to note that not every professional associations and professional organizations requires an exam for the purposes of recertification or professional certification renewal. Whether the professional certification includes an administered exam is not necessarily a determining factor of whether the professional associations and professional organizations requires everything it should of its applicants to obtain the professional certification. For example, the International Society of Performance Improvement (ISPI) has a comprehensive assessment that utilizes work experience to make a determination if the individual meets the criteria for the professional certification. For those professional associations and professional organizationss that administer exams as one of the criteria for the professional certification, the most common assessments appear to include items 1–5, depending on the resources.

Optimizing Certification Preparation Resources

To ensure the individual is adequately prepared for the professional certification examinations, the person should plan to purchase professional certification materials. It is recommended to work with the professional associations and professional organizations and individuals who have been previously certified to obtain their recommendations on the most effective resources. While borrowing resources from people who have been certified is an option, the person needs to consider if utilizing others' resources is the best option.

- Books are usually marked up.
- The resources on loan may not be the latest version.
- There is always liability using other people's property.
- The person who is becoming certified should consider the necessity of starting a personal library to support ongoing education.

Sources for purchasing professional certification resources are:

- Professional associations and professional organizations
- Booksellers (i.e., Amazon.com, eBay, Albris, Barnes & Noble, etc.)
- People who have been certified previously
- The publisher of the professional certification materials

Study groups become popular among those seeking professional certification. It is a preferred option for some instead of attending instructor-led classes. This is because study groups:

- Are available at a reduced cost and sometimes free of charge
- Can be held on site, virtually, or a combination of the two
- Provide opportunities for professional networking

When facilitating study groups that are associated with a certification exam, documentation is important because it is subject to audit by the professional associations and professional organizations. Study group participation should use certificates for documenting engagement. For traceability, it is important to distinguish the different types of certificates:

- **Certificate of attendance (COA):** Confirms the dates and times a person attended the sessions of a course, course title, instructor, and institution.
- **Certificate of completion (COC):** States that a person has met the objectives of a course, completion date, course title, instructor, and institution.
- **Certificate of demonstration (COD):** If the person is required to demonstrate an ability to perform a specific task (i.e., on the job), then a COD may be appropriate. For example, cardiopulmonary resuscitation (CPR) needs to be simulated.
- **Certificate of enrollment (COE):** Verifies that a participant has paid fees and is scheduled to attend a specific course, course title, and institution (i.e., receipt).

- **Certificate of participation (COP):** Verifies a person was actively engaged in a course, dates and times a person attended the sessions of a course, course title, instructor, and institution.
- **Certificate of testing (COT):** Confirms that the individual completed a course, for instance, e-learning for which a test was given as part of the course and the person passed the threshold. So, if 80% is the passing grade, then the person is issued a certificate. For example, some applications will use the sharable content object reference model (SCORM), which is a collection of standards and specifications that uses XML to ensure the acceptability of test scores achieved by the learner, or the Aviation Industry Computer-Based Training Committee (AICC).

Determining Test-Taking Strategies

There are 20 myths regarding professional certification exams:

1. If the answer is obvious, it probably is a trick question.
2. Choosing the wrong answer will hurt your score more than leaving an answer blank.
3. Purchasing exam preparation materials is 100% assurance you will pass the exam.
4. The organization intends to limit the number of people who pass the certification exam.
5. Exam results are always provided at the completion of the exam.
6. Putting the exam off will make me more confident.
7. Your first choice answer when taking an exam is usually not the right answer.
8. The older you get, the harder it is to study for professional certification exams.
9. Many people fail their professional certification exams the first time.
10. All professional certification exams are created equally difficult.
11. Creating posters for formulas and charts is a silly idea.
12. Putting reminder charts on the refrigerator and on your nightstand is ineffective.
13. Exercising the night before the exam will not reduce stress.
14. Using your mobile phone as a study resource will not help.
15. Putting professional certification in your professional development plan is not necessary.
16. The survey you fill out before the exam determines the questions you get.
17. If you have more experience, you will get a harder exam.
18. If a topic area is answered incorrectly, the exam keeps asking you about that topic area until you get a specified number of questions right.
19. You get bonus points for completing a 4-hour exam early.
20. Demographic questions on the exam are not important.

Test-taking strategies will depend on the type of examination administered. From the aforementioned list, these appear to be tests that a strategy can be associated with:

- Written or computerized:
   - a. A standard test (i.e., multiple choice, true/false, yes/no, choose all that apply, drag and drop, matching, fill in the blank, etc.) is utilized 95% or more of the time due to the simplicity of utilizing many of questions and scoring.
   - b. Essay (not used often).
- A performance-based assessment/portfolio (projects completed) is utilized approximately 20% or more of the time due to direct relevance.
- Personality, attitude, or behavior analysis (utilized frequently).
- An oral examination (this can be performed through a panel of experts) is utilized less than 10% of the time.

For a written examination (essay):

- Answer the question and minimize extraneous content.
- Keep the responses as concise as possible.
- If permissible, use bullets.
- If permissible, use graphics and illustrations.

For an oral examination (panel responses):

- Answer the question and only the question.
- If the question is closed yes/no or true/false, keep it closed and only reply with yes/no or true/false.

For computer-based or paper-based questions that are yes/no or true/false:

- Generally, a positive choice is more likely to be true than a negative one.
- Generally, there tend to be more true or yes than false or no answers.
- Usually, the correct answer is the choice with the most information.
- Eliminate any items that seem like double negatives to eliminate trick questions.

For tests that are multiple choice:

- When you initially begin reviewing sample test questions (i.e., in professional certification review material through an exam simulator), look at all the questions (items) as normal, including correct and incorrect answers (distracters). Understand why the correct answer is the preferred choice. If the question has more than one correct answer, the exam question is based on the best answer, and there may be in fact more than one correct answer. Understand why the best answer should be chosen among multiple correct answers.

■ In your second review of the same set of test questions (i.e., in professional certification review material through printed flash cards), look at only the correct answers. This is because your brain has already been through the exercise on separating the right from the wrong questions already. Now, it is important to program your brain with only the correct answers.
■ Read the question fully (and aloud if necessary) before you look at the answer.
■ Think of the answer in your head before looking at the choices; this will help you gain confidence and confirm that you really know the answer to the question.
■ Eliminate answers you know are not right by using a pen and marking off as necessary.
■ Read each choice one by one before choosing your answer.

For tests that have more than one choice (multiple-multiple choice or select all that apply):

■ All of the above could be an option
■ None of the above might be an option
■ Some of the above: choose two of four (i.e., A and B of A, B, C, D) may also be an option

Tests that are administered in an attempt to determine behavioral competencies might include instruments such as:

■ Myers-Briggs
■ DISC (Dominance, Inducement, Submission, Compliance)
■ Amiable-expressive-analytical-driver

Some might ask why there are behavioral components to professional certification. The answer surrounds the importance of behavioral competencies as a significant component of the professional certification.

For exams that are behavioral in nature that look to evaluate attitude and behavior, some of the items that require concentration and preparation include:

■ Body language (nonverbal communication): is interpreted during the oral examination. Your gestures should be neutralized to ensure the right message is communicated (see Table 3.2).
■ Paralinguistics (tone): This is the manner in which something is expressed, including the amplitude, resonation, and other attributes of the voice, such as pausing.

Table 3.2 Nonverbal Communication Chart for Use in Verbal Examination

Nonverbal Communication Behavior/Gesture		*Observer's Interpretation*
Hands	Hand rubbing	Anticipating
	Palms open	Sincere
	Biting fingernails	Nervous
	Steepled fingers	Exerting authority
	Tugging ear with thumb and index finger	Indecisive
	Stroking chin	Trying to make decision
	Index finger on cheek/thumb under chin	Contemplating
	Scratching head	Lacking self-confidence
	Rubbing eye	Disbelief
	Tapping fingers	Impatience
	Pinching nose	Negative thought
	Hands on hips	Aggression
Head	Head tilted forward	Problem hearing
	Head tilted downward	Disbelief
Eyes	Direct eye contact	Engaged
	Looking away in other direction	Disinterested
Legs	Sitting legs apart	Open, relaxed
	Legs crossed	Boredom
Arms	Arms crossed	Defensive
	Arms stretched upward	Exhausted, finished talking
Feet	Quick walk	Confidence
	Feet tapping	Boredom
Paralinguistics/Tone/Other Voice Attributes		*Observer's Interpretation*
Voice	Talking faster	Nervous/forceful

(Continued)

Table 3.2   Nonverbal Communication Chart for Use in Verbal Examination (Continued)

Voice	Speaking slower	To ensure clarity
Voice	Raising voice	Making a point
Voice	Lowering voice	Calming down
Voice	Stuttering	Nervous
Lips	Hard closed: hmmm	Doubting
Teeth	Closed: grinding	Frustrated
Teeth	Closed: breathing through	Upset
Throat	Clearing throat	In disagreement
Mouth	Sighing	Disbelief
Mouth	Laughing	Feeling of mutual comfort
Tongue	Odd tongue movements or strange sounds	Tired, sick, or thirsty
	Mood/Emotions	*Observer's Interpretation*
Facial	Somewhat quiet smiling (softly)	Seeking agreement
Facial	Very quiet, not smiling	Serious, drawing conclusions
Facial	Somewhat quiet, frowning (softly)	Sick, not feeling well
Facial	Very quiet, frowning	Angry
Voice	Somewhat loud	Wanting to be heard
Voice	Very loud	In disagreement

■ Mood: This conveys feelings of being happy, sad, serious, or joyful and is actually separate from body language and something that is also important to keep in check.

Overcoming Anxiety and Mental Blocks

Test anxiety is a combination of negative physical and mental complications that occur before and during the period of a certification exam. The feelings that are experienced include:

- Headache
- Upset stomach
- Impatience
- Fear of failure
- Worry
- Crying
- Yelling
- Vomiting
- Trembling or shaking
- Lack of feeling of self-worth
- Self-depreciating thoughts
- Dramatic rise or drop in emotions
- Shortness of breath

Certification exam anxiety is real for many people and nothing to play with. Measures need to be put into place to reduce and if possible eliminate exam anxiety. Test anxiety is prevalent among students of all ages and has been an object of study since the early 1950s, beginning with researchers George Mandler and Seymour Sarason.

The keys to overcoming test anxiety need to be simple:

- Understand you are not unique regarding test anxiety: It is a common problem.
- Pray or meditate to gain internal confidence.
- Let people around you know how tense you are feeling and ask for support.
- Avoid foods that create nervous tension (i.e., coffee and sweets).
- Find ways to relax and take your mind off the exam.
- Keep in mind you can retake the exam in the future.
- Understand if you do fail, you will not be the first or the last.

Mental blocks are related to exam anxiety but are different. A mental block is anything that prohibits the person from following through with certification. Examples include:

- Passing the certification exam
- Locating a certification exam center that is conveniently located
- Finding a convenient time to take the certification exam
- Identifying a study group with friendly people who are easy to study with
- Obtaining PDUs/CEUs to maintain certification
- Investing the money to pay for the certification exam because the employer will not

- Disliking a member in the association so you do not go to meetings
- Having a bad experience with the association's customer service becomes a turnoff

There are keys to overcoming a mental block:

- Write it down and acknowledge it is a mental block.
- Refuse to accept it as an obstacle going forward.

One of the keys to avoiding mental blocks is to avoid going the certification journey on your own. An accountability partner is any individual or group who will encourage you to stay on course with your certification program. These individuals include:

- Members of the study group who are also preparing for certification
- Local chapter members
- Local chapter board of directors
- Your supervisor, who may have a vested interest in your completing the certification
- Family members
- Project team members
- People in your work group who may pursue certification in the future

Some of the characteristics of good accountability partners are:

- They understand what you are going through.
- It will not appear to be an inconvenience for them to help you.
- They never discourage you by saying you will not pass the exam.
- They offer to study with you (i.e., use flash cards, role play, etc.).
- They make sure you do not become overstressed with the certification process.
- They celebrate the success with you when the exam is over and you have passed.

There are ways to find accountability partners:

- Visit the local chapter meetings.
- Visit professional association websites and look for study group partners.
- Find individuals who have been certified previously and ask them to be a mentor.

Completing the Readiness Assessment

Before you sit for your certification exam, do not be surprised if you get many people asking you, "Are you ready?" A readiness assessment is an evaluation of the prospective certificant's capabilities to achieve the certification. In other words, it attempts primarily to determine if the person will pass the exam. Other readiness assessments may go a step further to determine if the person will be able to maintain the certification. The readiness assessment is the last step that should be taken before finalizing your examination date.

Finalizing an examination date is technically different from scheduling an examination date. Finalizing the examination date is a mental process that involves confirming the examination date. It is *casting in stone* when the certification exam will be taken. Scheduling the certification exam is letting the professional associations and professional organizations know when you *intend* to take the exam. Scheduling the certification exam can usually be changed, most times for free (at least once) or at a small fee. You usually do not have to give a reason for changing your examination date. If there is any question regarding your desire to change your date, be honest and state that you did not feel ready, were nervous, or had competing priorities on that date. *Note:* Even when an exam date has been finalized, there are circumstances that can arise that require a new exam date.

Some professional associations and professional organizations do a good job with readiness assessments, and others miss this important step in the process. Novell is an example of a company that does a good job in certification readiness by using what they refer to as a technical skills assessment (TSA). The prospective certificant can go on its website and access a sample examination. The website provides answers to frequently asked questions that make understanding readiness a smooth process.

Suggested Reading

American Society for Quality (ASQ). (2009). *Quality Body of Knowledge (QBOK)*. Milwaukee, WI: American Society for Quality.

The Association for Operations Management (APICS). (2009). *Operations Management Body of Knowledge (OMBOK)*. Chicago: APICS, Association for Operations Management.

Kurpius, S., and Stafford, M. (2006). *Testing and Measurement*. Thousand Oaks, CA: Sage.

Ory, J., and Ryan, K. (1993). *Tips for Improving Testing and Grading*. Newbury Park, CA: Sage.

Project Management Institute. (2013). *Project Management Body of Knowledge (PMBOK Guide)*. Newtown Square, PA: Project Management Institute.

Chapter 4

Achieving Professional Certification

Key Lessons

- Ready, Set, Go
- Career Planning
- Out of High School or with a General Equivalency Diploma
- Picking Up One- and Two-Year Programs
- Continuing on to the Four-Year Degree
- Stretching to Advanced Degrees
- Terminal Degrees and Beyond
- Practice Analysis
- Competency Development
- Learning Methodologies
- Capacity Building
- Day of the Certification Exam
- Publicizing the Credential
- Updating the Résumé, CV, Portfolio, and Biography
- Applying for New Positions

Ready, Set, Go

It is the start of the amazing certification race, and you feel in first place:

- Someone has agreed to help pay for your certification exam fees.

- You found some friend to study with to avoid the certification prep course costs.
- You have developed meaningful relationships with the professional associations or professional organizations.
- The certification you are pursuing is in high demand.
- You are fully comfortable with the body of knowledge.
- You seem to know the vast majority of the answers to the online sample tests.
- A competitor calls about a higher-paying job and would like to consider you for it.
- Your peers are looking up to you with respect.
- Your family is behind you with full support.

Career Planning

Everyone needs a career plan. A career plan helps you determine your skills, abilities, and professional interests; what career best suits your short- and long-term objectives; and what training and development you will need for your chosen occupation. It is never too early to start a career plan. In fact, some parents begin putting ideas into the minds of their children at a very early age. Moreover, some children make decisions early in life regarding what career they will actually pursue.

Everyone can benefit from a career planner. A career planner is someone who is professionally trained and can give guidance and direction to those people needing consultation on jobs. There are different types of people who serve in the capacity of career planners, including:

- School counselors
- Recruiters (also called headhunters)
- Outplacement services
- Talent management professionals
- Training and development specialists
- Human resource (HR) practitioners
- Psychologists
- Résumé writers
- Personal coaches and mentors
- Teachers and professors
- Peers who serve as role models
- Succession planners

Choosing a good career planner is perhaps one of the most important life decisions. Good career planners will go to whatever lengths necessary to provide:

- Psychological reinforcement and encouragement that the person can succeed
- Ongoing coaching and mentoring to ensure the person understands how to document his or her education
- Development plans that will provide a road map of what the person needs to focus on in terms of certifications, degrees, and the like to meet the requirements of the desired job
- Assessments that identify the interests and skills of the individuals
- Market data that show job trends and changes in the market
- Job leads and references so the person understands how to search for employment

Some of the activities that encourage a career plan are:

- Have the person express what most interests him or her
- Consult family and friends who have held that career position to talk to the person
- Expose the person to different types of related careers so the person understands the options
- Go to career fairs so the individual obtains a real sense of the long lines and complexity
- Ask the person what he or she wants to be when grown up, even if the person is grown up
- Point out examples of people who have chosen the career path and are happy in it and gather testimonials if at all possible
- Help the person understand that he or she may decide to change his or her career and, if so, what a second and third choice would be
- Show the person the results of not being actively involved in career planning (i.e., ending up in a job he or she will dislike, frequent job changes, and possibly unemployment)

People must understand that careers are subject to change. People should also realize that a job is only a job. There are 168 hours in a week. A job is only a part of life, maybe 25% at best, assuming an 8-hour workday or 40 hours of work per week. Life is about choices, sense of purpose, and what people feel led to do at the time. Some industries will flourish for a while and then will be less in demand due to changes in technology or the work being performed elsewhere. So, career choices should be as portable or transferable as possible. For this purpose, many choose college as a foundation, and certification becomes reinforcement to that foundation.

Here is a sensitive topic, but it is worth discussing. Going to college full time directly after high school is a good decision for many people. Other good decisions might involve choosing a career in the military, sports, government, religion, and other areas. Some individuals may not desire to go to college but must understand all options for education (i.e., certification) and find the path that suits their skills, ability, desire, and career objectives. This said, a person can be encouraged to go to college directly after high school; however, this option does not appeal and work for everyone. This is where certification can come into play for many people. The worst spot to be in is "I don't know what I want to do for a living."

Why does this happen?

- Lack of career planning, which may be the fault of the educational system (i.e., public high school) and counselors who do not work with the student to explore all available options
- Lack of access to the right people currently holding careers in specific areas so the student receives enough information to make decisions about what career to pursue
- Lack of clarity in the mind of the student, so the student struggles to make a good decision

Out of High School or with a General Equivalency Diploma

The minimum level of education for most certifications is a high school education or general equivalency diploma (GED). Many certification programs that allow certificants to only have a high school education require more work experience. For example, the project management professional (PMP) certification requires 7,500 work experience hours for a person who has only a high school education compared to 4,500 work experience hours for an individual with a college degree. So, those who have not achieved a 2- or 4-year degree should expect more rigorous requirements for some certifications.

Why would someone pursue certification right out of high school instead of achieving a college degree?

- The person is uncertain of what career to choose after high school and so perceives that pursuing certification will help him or her to enter the job market immediately.
- The time it takes to achieve certification is months instead of years.
- The cost of certification is less than a achieving a degree.
- The person may not have been admitted to the school of choice, so certification becomes a desirable option.
- It is generally easier to become admitted to a certification program than to a degree program.

In what arenas does certification work for people who have achieved a high school diploma or GED?

- Information technology fields
- Technical support, mechanical, or industrial jobs
- Apprentice and internship-type positions that have staged progression

Picking Up One- and Two-Year Programs

After a person has completed high school or obtained a GED, the person may decide to pursue:

- Technical school
- Community college

Some examples of technical schools are:

- The Universal Technical Institute Incorporated (UTI) is accredited by the ACCSC (Accrediting Commission of Career Schools and Colleges) and provides, nationwide, technical education training for students seeking careers in automotive, diesel, collision repair, motorcycle, and marine technician fields. At a technical school such as UTI, there is targeted training in the field where the students will work. Certificates are usually given at the end of successful completion of training courses. These individuals then are regarded as certified technicians.
- Sometimes, technical schools and community colleges collaborate. For example, the Michigan Technical Education Center (MTEC) and Kalamazoo Valley Community College (KVCC) offer academy programs for careers that involve corrections officers, hospitality, mechatronic systems technicians, patient care, police work, production technicians, utility line workers, and wind turbine technicians. On successful completion of these collaborative programs, depending on whether it is issued from the technical school or community college and field of study, the student will receive either a certificate (e.g., from the technical school) or associate's degree (e.g., from the community college).
- Students who attend a traditional community college, such as Rockland Community College in Suffern, New York, will earn an associate's degree or, if not enough credits for an associate's degree, they will earn credits to be applied to a bachelor's degree to be achieved elsewhere.

Continuing on to the Four-Year Degree

The 4-year degree (alone) has come to represent a dilemma for some graduates and employers. Many who earn a bachelor's degree are unable to find the desired job in their field due to the overwhelming number of individuals in the job market with a similar degree. Moreover, a bachelor's degree alone may not impress many employers as it once did 20 years ago. There are two types of bachelor's degrees:

■ A bachelor of arts (BA) degree is humanities based. It provides a balanced liberal arts education and general knowledge in a recognized discipline.
■ A bachelor of science (BS) degree is science based. It provides a balanced liberal arts education and a scientific, technical, or professional level of knowledge.

It is important to keep in mind that many who have bachelor's degrees are not right out of college. They may have completed their bachelor's degree later in life, have joined the military and been on a different educational plan, or have earned multiple bachelor's degrees instead of pursuing an advanced degree. To strengthen the bachelor's programs, some students have used these approaches:

■ **Having a major and a minor:** A minor requires half the credits (16–20) of a major. Many liberal arts colleges support a major and a minor.
■ **Having a double degree:** Johns Hopkins University and the Peabody Institute, for example, address the double-degree dilemma for those students who are challenged with selecting one course of study or have talents and interests in two areas.
■ **Having a major and professional certification:** This appears to be the optimal solution for some individuals (i.e., obtaining a business degree and a supply chain management certification).

Stretching to Advanced Degrees

A significant number of those who have earned bachelor's degrees in popular fields such as business, education, psychology, and the like are finding it necessary to continue their education and pursue advanced degrees. There are primarily three types of advanced degrees:

■ Master's degree: It usually takes 1 to 2 years beyond the bachelor's degree and demands a higher level of commitment. It is granted to individuals who have completed study in a specific area and demonstrate mastery over the content. There are two types of master's degrees:
  – A master of arts (MA) degree.
  – A master of science (MS) degree.
■ Doctoral degree: The doctoral is a high-level degree that usually comes after the master's degree. It is work intensive and frequently requires full-time dedication. There are some programs that cater to working professionals and allow courses during the evenings. Most doctorates are achieved by

researching a unique topic under a dissertation committee. Earning a doctorate typically takes 3 to 5 years. People pursue a PhD (doctor of philosophy) if they are interested in becoming a college professor, author, or expert in a field.

■ Professional degree: The professional degree is required for working in medicine, science, or law. Students can pursue a professional degree after achieving a bachelor's or master's degree. It can take 3 to 5 years to pursue occupations in law and 3 to 10 years to complete careers in the scientific or medical fields due to requirements for residency and the like. There are first professional degrees and advanced professional degrees.

Coupling professional certification with an advanced degree can be a winning combination (i.e., MBA and a Certified Quality Engineer [CQE] combination).

Terminal Degrees and Beyond

A terminal degree is a term used in the United States to refer to the highest academic degree in a field of study. It is a term that people outside the United States may not use. A terminal degree means that you technically can go no further with education in that area. Terminal degrees usually happen at the PhD level, but in some disciplines occur at the master's level (i.e., master of architecture [MArch]) if there is no PhD program currently available.

Postdoctoral research (postdoc) is scholarly research conducted by a person who obtained a doctorate (PhD). A postdoc is normally completed within 5 years. The student is referred to as a postdoctoral fellow or scholar. Fellows and scholars agree to conduct research under the guidance of an expert for a number of years.

Another option for terminal degrees is the dual PhD and law degree program. For example, Cornell University offers a 6-year dual PhD/JD (juris doctor) developmental psychology and law program. It is designed to prepare the next generation of professionals who work on the issues concerning the law, psychology, and human development. This program from a top-ranked university boasts experimental focus, academic excellence, favorable timeline, and intellectual support.

Of course, it is not sensible to compare a terminal degree to certification. However, what is worth further analysis is the amount of time a person will invest in education beyond the terminal degree and then compare that to the value of certification. For example, many attorneys are now becoming educated in legal project management and becoming certified in project management. Practice analysis is the recommended industry approach to determine the path to follow.

Practice Analysis

Practice analysis, job analysis, or role delineation study:

- is the systematic study of an occupation and the roles and responsibilities of those employed
- involves surveying those in the occupation around the world in the discipline to determine the knowledge, skills, and abilities that are relevant to the profession
- information is used to identify competencies required to effectively carry out the job function
- has become an integral part of a professional certification program

Arbet, Lathrop, and Hooker (2009) join the bandwagon and discuss how practice analysis has been used to improve the certifying examinations for physician assistants. This represents the correct way to do things by obtaining input from those previously certified (and in some cases not certified but still experienced in the occupation) to improve the professional certification process. professional associations or professional organizations should work in conjunction with industry experts to carry out practice analysis approximately every 3 to 5 years. The task inventory, which is a component of practice analysis, details the functions the individual performs on the job. For example, a supply chain management professional may be involved with logistics, transportation, warehousing, and distribution.

As a position matures, the task inventory may increase. As the task inventory increases, the compensation is subject to increase, thereby increasing qualifications for the position. Qualification increases are frequently met through professional certification since the requirement for an advanced degree represents a larger stretch by comparison.

Competency Development

There is a saying that what gets measured gets done. In other words, if it is worth doing, then it is worth measuring. To develop competencies, they first have to be measured. The previous discussion of practice analysis touched the tip of the iceberg. Whether you are an employee or manager, we are all directly responsible for defining our job role in terms of effectiveness and efficiency. We look at not only how well we perform activities but also for ways to streamline processes by doing more with less. We are tasked with working smarter and using the resources at our disposal in a manner that supports the organization and project objectives as a whole.

Defining which competencies are essential to be successful in an organization can help:

- Recruit and retain the right staff

- Ensure people demonstrate the desired expertise
- Evaluate performance more effectively
- Create targeted action plans to improve performance
- Customize learning and development to meet the needs of the individual
- Strategize more appropriately to address business continuity and succession planning
- Deal with change more resiliently
- Promote professional certification programs more concretely

As discussed in Chapter 1, competencies (both behavioral and technical) are core, common, and critical to a professional certification program. Competency development should be viewed as an ongoing process that should last throughout an individual's career. It not only should help a person realize his or her potential but also should keep the person up to date on changing trends in the industry.

For this reason, there are performance evaluations that seek to determine how well the person met his or her annual objectives. Going one step further, there needs to be a development planning process in place that focuses on helping the individual embrace continuous improvement. professional certification programs become an integral part of that process.

A buzzword that has been hitting the airwaves is competency development framework (CDF). What is it? Think of CDF as a tool that outlines the behaviors and skills that people are required to have for a specific position. If the person desires a new position, for instance, then the person is required to demonstrate those competencies to be considered for the role. The following three characteristics are important for a formalized CDF:

- **Practice analysis/role delineation study:** Begin with a strong foundation from the industry; in this way, there is a level playing field that will not likely be disputed.
- **Involve the right subject matter experts (SMEs):** Managers, employees, and perhaps an external consultant will be required to verify the practice analysis and support the design and continuous enhancement to the CDF
- **Formalize the process in the HR systems:** If it is not documented, then it did not happen. So, it is critically important that desired competencies are agreed on and tracked. Performance evaluation is a common module in most every HR system. However, competency development also falls under the umbrella of development planning. Where performance evaluation looks at meeting objectives, development planning is what the person can do to continuously improve through coaching, mentoring, shadowing, training, and other growth opportunities. Where performance evaluation looks at what they did, development planning focuses on what they are capable of doing, their potential.

The tools that work well for setting up a CDF are obviously from a human resources information system (HRIS). This should be basic functionality for any robust HRIS. Those who have not yet implemented an HRIS will need to set up a project plan to address this initiative.

1. Seek endorsement from senior management.
2. Begin by setting up a team for the CDF. It is hoped HR will be part of the team.
3. Set up the means by which information on competencies will be collected and distributed. Web-based surveys and a centralized e-mail box (i.e., competencydevelopment@abccorp.com) might work well for this purpose.
4. Establish how information will be reviewed and stored. Create a template (i.e., in Microsoft Excel) and save it to a repository (i.e., Microsoft SharePoint).
5. Then, begin piloting the system to see it work. Keep in mind that linking work performance to demonstration of a competency can take several forms:

- Manager review: done periodically and at an annual performance evaluation
- Peer review: 360 feedback
- Third-party review: by customers, suppliers, or other key stakeholders

Professional certification comes into play by enabling more opportunities for the person to demonstrate the competency. What is nice is that the professional associations or professional organizations as an objective third party can provide verification, in fact, that the person has demonstrated this competency. For example, the person becomes certified as an Agile project manager from Project Management Institute (PMI). However, a question arises regarding the degree of competence in managing large-scale Agile projects. A possible solution might be to assign projects in increasing complexity. This gradual approach may be in the best interest of the individual and organization for competency growth.

Learning Methodologies

The adult learning theory (notice this is not the adult training theory) should be utilized when helping professionals to learn. The two options to transfer information are:

- **Deliver training:** Material is provided in one form or another (pushed, i.e., as a presentation) or accessed by the individual (pulled, i.e., from a website).
- **Enable learning:** Content is made available, experiences are shared, observations are made, or knowledge is transferred.

Some of the key characteristics of the adult learning theory are:

- Adults want to be respected and have their comments considered.
- Adults need to participate in small-group activities during the learning.
- Adult learners come to learning with previous experiences and knowledge.
- Transfer of learning for adults is not automatic and requires facilitation.
- Adult learners need concrete experiences in which they apply learning to their job.
- Adults need feedback on how they are doing and the results of their efforts.
- Adults like following processes and systems and learning in modules.
- Adults need clear objectives and continuity to avoid frustration.

The four stages of learning that apply to adults are:

- Unconscious incompetence (novice): don't know what they don't know.
- Conscious incompetence (apprentice): know what they don't know.
- Consciously competent (journeyman): know what they know.
- Unconscious competence (master): don't know what they know.

The environments in which adults are trained or learn best (use this as a checklist) have these characteristics:

- Are well organized
- Are conducive to learning (i.e., the room has the appropriate level of heating and air conditioning)
- Are project based with a definite beginning and end
- Exhibit timeliness (start on time and end on time)
- Provide relevance to their role and responsibilities
- Have clarity of message/agenda
- Indicate action items/next steps
- Must effectively enable and sustain communication
- Support collaboration and teamwork
- Encourage open, honest, direct, and transparent discussion
- Use reliable media (i.e., web conferencing for virtual audiences)
- Should eliminate or minimize all sources of noise:
  - Physical noise (i.e., traffic)
  - Disruptions (i.e., issues that cause unexpected delays)
  - Physical noise (cross talk)
- Create opportunities for team learning
- Provide access to refreshments
- Provide engaging activities that prevent falling asleep
- Promote collaboration
- Present handouts to minimize note taking

- Be on site or optimize virtual media
- Be facilitated by a leader or moderator

The different modes of delivering training are:

- Instructor led (in person)
- Instructor led (webinar conferencing)
- Instructor led (recorded and rebroadcast on-demand webinars)
- Group workshop (study group)
- Practice simulation (not on the job)
- On-the-job training
- E-learning (computer-based training)
- Manuals (written documentation)

The different modes of engaging learning (in combination with training) are:

- Observation checklist
- Case study review
- Role plays
- Interactive discussion boards
- Company tours
- Benchmarking
- Competitive analyses
- Counseling
- Mentoring
- Coaching
- Shadowing
- Peer-to-peer relationships

Capacity Building

Capacity building is an ongoing process through which organizations (i.e., companies, businesses, and institutions) enhance their ability to identify and meet development challenges for their members and employees. Developmental challenges might include maintaining up-to-date expertise required to stay competitive in the global marketplace. Capacity building proposes to understand the obstacles that have an impact on individuals and organizations. It is concerned with what can be done to help people realize their potential through growth initiatives. Capacity building looks to implement and enhance programs, processes, and systems that will enable measurable and sustainable results. It includes, but is not limited to, the accumulation and transfer of knowledge through educational initiatives such as professional certification.

Both professional associations or professional organizations and institutions that support professional certification are concerned with capacity building. Competency development and capacity building go hand in hand. As an organization strengthens its competencies, it builds capacity. Some of the potential benefits of building capacity include:

■ Improved organizational learning
■ Increased change resilience
■ Enhanced job satisfaction, thereby supporting employee retention
■ Change management initiatives support
■ Strengthened competitive positions
■ Education of people at a higher level
■ Movement of people out of their comfort zone into the stretch zone
■ Continuous improvement philosophy enabled

Day of the Certification Exam

For the day of the certification exam, it first should be obvious to get plenty of sleep the night before. Physical and emotional health are good because the way you feel physically and mentally will have an impact on your exam performance.

Here are the logistics:

■ Arrival: Come to the test center at least 15 minutes early. This will enable you to select the preferred seating location and have any last-minute questions answered.
■ Restroom facilities: Use the restroom before walking into the exam room. There are strict guidelines regarding leaving and reentering the exam room. When you exit the exam room, you become suspect regarding why you are doing so.
■ Meal: Eat before the test an item that digests easily and does not make you too full (i.e., cereal, yogurt, fruit, donut, etc.).
■ Identification: Bring two forms of identification, at a minimum a driver's license and credit card.
■ Calculator: A normal functioning calculator is usually permitted. It is good to keep one in your car in case the testing center does not provide it.
■ Blank paper: Blank paper is a must to bring along; it may be preferable to immediately transfer content to blank paper on entering the testing center (i.e., formulas).
■ Tissues: Sinus problems can affect thinking ability, so having a small pack of tissue is a good plan.
■ Beverages: Although coffee usually contains caffeine, it has a tendency to increase nervousness; a better choice may be water.

- Candy: Hard candy is usually preferred over gum. Gum can potentially pull out a tooth filling; it can sound loud and be distracting.
- Snacks: Food many times is not permitted and can cause the stomach to become upset.

On completion of the exam:

- Confirm with the testing center that nothing else needs to be signed or recorded.
- If you did not immediately receive your pass/fail test scores, inquire again about them.
- On receipt of your passing score, notify the professional association chapter by e-mail. This is important because it may not receive immediate notification that you obtained the professional certification. Professional association chapters frequently put recognition into place to acknowledge those newly certified at the upcoming chapter meeting, via the website, or via trade publications.
- Do not discuss any of the exam content with anyone. It can be interpreted as cheating and could be grounds for disallowing your professional certification. It is considered an ethics violation.
- Celebrate with family and friends.
- Send thank you notes to the individuals who have been supportive.
- Notify your employer.
- Let the people in the study group know.
- Send a thank you note to the publisher to acknowledge that the professional certification study materials were effective in helping you successfully pass the exam. Also, give the publisher any recommendations on how to improve the materials.
- File professional certification certification study materials so they can be reused by anyone else. Return any professional certification study materials that have been borrowed from someone else.
- Log into the professional association website and ensure that your professional certification has been recorded in their system.
- Confirm with the professional associations or professional organizations on the phone when you will receive your professional certification letter.

Note: If you fail the exam, do the necessary research to determine if there was a scoring error. Many professional associations or professional organizations have reported experiences with scoring errors.

Publicizing the Credential

According to research conducted by Knapp International (2007), the top three benefits cited by individuals achieving professional certification were:

1. Enhanced credibility
2. Personal satisfaction of attaining goal
3. Recognition by peers and professional colleagues

That same study stated that the top three advantages of professional certification to employers are:

1. Independent verification of knowledge/competency
2. Increased productivity/efficiency
3. Higher quality of work

So, when should the publicity for the professional certification begin?

1. This could be after receipt of the confirmation from the professional associations or professional organizations. This confirmation may occur via e-mail or may be at the testing center after examination.
2. If a professional association is issuing the professional certification, then accepting the credential can be done at the professional association chapter event. This is important because peer recognition is important to the professional association and the professional certification recipient. It is a common practice for the professional association to award the newly certified individual a pin.
3. The professional association can provide additional visibility for the newly certified individual with write-ups on the website and in the chapter newsletter.
4. The national professional association may provide visibility for professional certification recipients in its trade journal or on its website.
5. The professional association should encourage the newly certified individual to become an active volunteer and consider serving on the board of directors (BOD) for the local chapter.

Care and consideration should go into publicizing the credential. On the one hand, the newly certified individual wants to inform many people of the accomplishment. This is great and appropriate. On the other hand, the newly certified person must keep in mind political sensitivity associated with the new certification. Some suggestions for publicizing the credential are provided next. Some approaches will work better than others depending on the circumstances.

1. The certificant should let his or her immediate supervisor know first and ask for the manager's agreement on how the new certification should be publicized. The manager may take the lead on this by sending out a broadcast communication, which is more preferred than the certificant doing it.
2. Ask the manager to note the completion of the certification in the certificant's HR file. It is hoped this was previously established as a development objective, which will add more significance to the achievement of the certification.

3. The person should have his or her manager contact the company's media relations department and request visibility in the upcoming company newsletter or on its website.
4. The certificant should ask for the correct protocol regarding contacting external media (i.e., local, state, or national press).
5. The certificant may want to ask the certifying agency (i.e., information technology vendor) or association if there are other ways of publicizing the credential.
6. New business cards and stationary can feature the designation at the end of the name.
7. The certificant should proudly display the credential on a plaque on the office or cubicle wall.
8. The manager of the certificant can arrange for a group luncheon so that people can officially recognize and celebrate the credential.

Updating the Résumé, Curriculum Vitae, Portfolio, and Biography

Revising the résumé after achieving certification is a good idea. The following tips can improve the representation of the certificant's job experience. The changed résumé should do the following:

■ The credential should be incorporated in the certificant's name (i.e., John Doe, PMP).
■ If an executive summary or career objective statement is used at the beginning of the résumé, compliment this description with the certification.
■ Create two versions of the résumé, a short version and a long version. Some employers will prefer to see a one- or two-page résumé, and others will want lots of detail.
■ Include a summary of projects within the résumé or in the long version.
■ If multiple positions are held (i.e., a second part-time job as an adjunct faculty member), list the second position on a separate page in the long-version résumé.
■ If there is a profile in a social networking site (i.e., LinkedIn, Facebook, or Twitter), consider providing the link to that website.
■ Be action-oriented, listing roles, responsibilities, and accomplishments.
■ Avoid weak verbs (i.e., participated in, was involved with, etc.).
■ Use power verbs (i.e., directed, led, remediated, restored, organized, controlled, etc.).
■ Scan the certification certificate and consider including it when applying for another position. Many résumé engines allow addition of attachments.

- Use bullets and short one-sentence explanations.
- If many acronyms are used, consider a supplemental section that defines these terms.
- Consider adding a section for skills summary or competencies.
- Review role delineation studies or practice analyses to determine if the competencies identified on the résumé reflect industry expectations for the position.

The difference between a résumé and a curriculum vitae (CV) is the amount of information.

- A résumé is a summary of education, work experience, and skills (one to two pages).
- A CV is usually three or more pages and provides a detailed synopsis. It includes a summary of education, work experience, skills, teaching and research conducted, publications, presentations, speaking engagements, awards, honors, affiliations, and more.
  - In Europe, the Middle East, Africa, or Asia, employers may expect a CV.
- In the United States, employers may expect to receive a CV when applying for certain positions (i.e., academic, scientific, or research, fellowships, or grants).

A portfolio is a collection of documents that support items mentioned on the résumé or CV. The portfolio should be scanned as a PDF file so they cannot be modified and can be e-mailed:

- Certificates
- Transcripts
- Letters of reference
- Publications
- Performance reviews
- Work products (i.e., project dashboards or training programs, such as e-learning created)

A biography is a half-page to one-page summary of:

- Work experience
- Education
- Achievements
- Professional Affiliations (i.e., membership in professional associations)

Individuals who have achieved professional certification should seriously consider the advantages of maintaining all four:

- Résumé: May have both a short and long version.

- Short version: It should list the current role and previous role and document up to 10 years. Some job applications will desire to see the past four employers. The sections should include work experience, education, awards/recognition, professional associations, and profile summary.
  - Long version: It should document the past four employers, which may represent up to 20 years. Some job applications will desire to see work experience since college (2- or 4-year degree). The sections should include work experience, education, awards/recognition, professional associations, certification/certificates, special projects/community involvement, and profile summary.
- CV: The sections should minimally include work experience, education, publications, awards/recognition, professional associations, presentations (speaking engagements), research (scholarly works), special projects/community involvement, travel experience, languages spoken if more than one (living in other countries), and profile summary.
- Portfolio: Includes letters of reference, certifications, certificates of completion, books, published articles, work products completed, awards/recognition, copies of presentations and speaking engagements, samples of training created, and the like.
- Biography: A one-paragraph to one-page summary, depending on instrumental use, that should include main accomplishments in reverse chronological order, work experience, education, certifications/certificates, and professional associations. As appropriate, a professional picture adds a personal touch.

Applying for New Positions

When applying for new positions, it is common online and in written applications to see a series of questions that are targeted toward certification. The following are some examples:

- Do you have a professional license or certification? Yes/No
- When did you obtain this certification or license? _____
- Who issued the certification or license? _____
- If you have a license or certification, has it been subject to discipline, including censure, suspension, revocation, or probation, in any state or jurisdiction? Yes/No
- If you have a license or certification, has it ever been denied for renewal, have you surrendered your license in lieu of discipline, or have you surrendered a license/certification in any state or jurisdiction? Yes/No

- If you have a professional license or certification, are you aware of any pending discipline or complaints filed against your license/certification with any regulatory board in any state or jurisdiction? Yes/No
- What is the certification or license number? _____
- Which authority issues the certification or license? _____

Some of the more popular certifications are stored in the online database and may require clicking on a search button to locate them. In some online systems, if the certification cannot be located through the search function, it may not be possible to list the certification separately. In these cases, the certification should be listed in the résumé or CV. When possible, it is appropriate to spell out the certification, for instance, project management professional (PMP), and include the entity associated with the certification, in this instance the Project Management Institute (PMI).

Suggested Reading

Arbet, S., Lathrop, J., and Hooker, R., (2009). Using practice analysis to improve the certifying examinations for professional organizations. *Journal of the American Academy of Physician Assistants* February. Retrieved December 11, 2012, from http://www.jaapa.com/using-practice-analysis-to-improve-the-certifying-examinations-for-pas/article/127551/.

Department of Human Development, Cornell University, College of Human Ecology. (n.d.). Dual PhD/JD Program. Retrieved February 21, 2013, from http://www.human.cornell.edu/hd/dual-phd-jd/index.cfm.

Knapp & Associates International. (2007). *Knapp Certification Industry Scan*. Princeton, NJ: Knapp International.

Peabody Institute, Johns Hopkins University. (2012). The Double Degree Dilemma. Retrieved February 16, 2013, from http://www.peabody.jhu.edu/conservatory/admissions/tips/doubledegree.html.

Project Management Institute. (2002). *Project Manager Competency Development Framework*. Newtown Square, PA: Project Management Institute.

Ricker, S. (2013). 5 Lessons from Your First Job to Apply to Your Entire Career. Retrieved February 17, 2013, from http://msn.careerbuilder.com/Article/MSN-3247-Career-Growth-and-Change-5-lessons-from-your-first-job-to-apply-to-your-entire-career/?SiteId=cbmsn43247&sc_extcmp=JS_3247_advice.

Chapter 5

Maintaining Professional Certification

Key Lessons

- Sustaining Professional Associations and Professional Organizations Certification Programs
- Budgeting Time, Energy, and Money
- Balancing Family, Friends, and Recreational Interests
- Earning PDUs and CEUs
- Volunteerism
- Obtaining Lifetime Professional Certification Status
- Reviving an Expired Professional Certification
- Sunsetting a Professional Certification that Has Been Retired
- Handling a Professional Certification that Becomes Problematic
- Reinstating a Professional Certification After It Has Been Revoked
- Deciding Not to Maintain Professional Certification

Sustaining Professional Association and Professional Organization Professional Certification Programs

In 2006, the American Society of Association Executives (ASAE) published the *7 Measures of Success: What Remarkable Associations Do That Others Don't*. This is a great book. It presents best-in-class ideas of organizations, such as the Society of Human Resource Management (SHRM), which reported record growth from

36,000 members in 1992 to over 250,000 today. How did SHRM do it? Perhaps more important, how does this organization retain members and continue to grow? The seven measures are:

1. A customer service culture: "We're here to serve you" approach.
2. Alignment of products and services with mission: Mission is central and products align.
3. Data-driven strategies: Gather, analyze, and use data to drive change.
4. Dialogue and engagement: Staff and volunteers engage on the professional association's direction and priorities.
5. Chief executive officer (CEO) as a broker of ideas: Facilitates visionary thinking throughout the association.
6. Organizational adaptability: Be willing to change and *not* to change.
7. Alliance building: Seek complimentary partners and projects.

Reportedly, only a portion of the revenue to support professional certification comes from grants or loans (i.e., from professional association headquarters). Percentagewise, only a small amount of contributions come through donations. Considering that the majority of professional associations currently absorb the cost associated with developing professional certification, they must depend on the membership to help sustain professional certification. Sustaining professional certification programs is done through membership dues and products and services to maintain the professional certification.

Due to changes in consumer demand, it has become a struggle for many professional certification programs.

According to research conducted by Knapp & Associates (2007), it is reported that nearly 40% of professional certification programs report little or no growth. However, more than 50% of those surveyed retain those individuals who have achieved the professional certification. It is interesting to note that approximately 90% of those who receive professional certification are required to engage in activities to maintain their credentials. So, part of the secret to survival appears to involve ensuring that those individuals who have achieved professional certification are retained and support continuous improvement in the professional certification program so that growth can be realized. This is especially important considering that the vast majority of professional certification programs require renewal or recertification every 3–5 years.

Professional certification is founded on the concept of goodwill, self-improvement, and other positivistic characteristics that makes it difficult to combat from an investment standpoint. Professional certification can be positioned to show tremendous value and offer flexibility, especially in those fields, such as project management, that are:

■ Intradisciplinary: within a discipline

- Interdisciplinary: between disciplines
- Transdisciplinary: across disciplines

It could be argued that professional certification protects the public and encourages compliance with regulatory authorities in addition to elevating the status of the professional associations or professional organizations. So, it makes sense why it is in their best interest to do everything possible to maintain professional certification programs. How does the professional association or professional organization encourage certificants to maintain the professional certification?

- Being invested in maturing the profession
- Through certification maintenance (CM) programs
- By instilling pride and accomplishment
- By competing for awards
- Promoting best practice
- By Benchmarking
- Through networking opportunities
- Through volunteering
- By becoming engaged in practice analysis
- By creating a philosophy of membership for life

How does the professional association or professional organization encourage the industry at large to support the professional certification?

- With market studies showing success cases
- By listing them in the job description as highly desirable
- By keeping the professional certification up to date
- By linking the professional certification to job performance
- By engaging the external agencies to become involved as sponsors
- By publishing content that adds value to the job market knowledge base
- By instilling motivation in its members to become volunteers

Budgeting Time, Energy, and Money

When a person achieves professional certification, the person has to keep in shape to maintain it. The best way to describe it is to think of it as exercise. Many certifications are established on the premise of studying a couple hours per month or 20 professional development units/continuing education units (PDUs/CEUs) per year. Some professional associations or professional organizations will schedule 2-hour chapter meetings once per month as a dinner from 6:00 to 8:00 p.m. or 7:00 to 9:00 p.m. One hour may be set aside for networking and the other hour for the program. This only allows the certificant to earn 1 PDU/CEU. However, if the professional associations or professional organizations has two programs in one evening (i.e., the main presentation and a bonus program), then the certificant can earn 2 PDUs/CEUs. The certificant would then most likely require a 2.5-hour meeting from 5:30 to 8:00 p.m. or 6:30 to 9:00 p.m. There may be 30 minutes set aside for networking and 2 hours for the programs, respectively, 1 hour each. Note that a 50- to 60-minute presentation is considered allowable for 1 PDU/CEU.

Energy is an important aspect of time investment because some certificants will be tired after work or may have other responsibilities that conflict with opportunities to earn PDUs/CEUs. professional associations or professional organizations can structure events so that certificants can attend virtually and pay a fee to attend the presentation. Attendance can be tracked by the webinar hosting vendor. An assessment can be administered for those virtual attendees to ensure they actively participated. Due to the trust system associated with participation, there should not be an overwhelming concern with a certificant who chose to attend virtually instead of in person. The rationale for allowing people to attend virtually and obtain PDUs/CEUs includes:

- Inability to drive to the location due to time constraints
- Inability for the person to attend due to health concerns or inclement weather
- Inability to attend due to lack of financial resources

Balancing Family, Friends, and Recreational Interests

There are some who, after achieving certification, may experience a new professional vacuum. This vacuum has a tendency to suck one into activities offered by the professional associations or professional organizations:

- Chapter meetings
- Special interest groups
- Meetings of the board of directors (BOD)
- Conferences
- Study group meetings
- Volunteer activities

Avoiding the temptation to become overinvolved initially is easier said than done because the new certificant is excited about the great achievement and is now with others who have pursued the same path. Some of the best relationships are made inside professional associations or professional organizations. This being said, if others now notice that the certificant has less time to spend with them, jealousy may occur. While it may seem small, it can create irritation over time. The best solution is to be open and honest and to seek agreement with those individuals, such as family, and come to an agreement about:

- The number of chapter meetings that will be attended, when, and where
- The new relationships that will likely occur as a result of achieving the professional certification and any members of the opposite gender if that creates an issue
- The amount of travel that is associated with volunteering
- The amount of financial investment (i.e., in going to chapter dinners) and if this is reimbursed by the company
- The change in feelings or attitude as a result of participating in the professional associations or professional organizations activities

Earning PDUs and CEUs

Earning PDUs or CEUs should be an enjoyable process. If it becomes burdensome, then there may be something lacking in the process. It becomes the responsibility of professional certification solutions providers to come up with creative ways to satisfy the educational needs of those who are maintaining professional certification. They need to work closely with the professional associations or professional organizations to understand the requirements for earning education hours. For example, some professional associations or professional organizations will accept a program that is a minimum of 50 minutes in duration as 1 PDU. Other professional associations or professional organizations will institute other criteria to define what qualifies as a PDU. The following are examples:

- Serving on the BOD for a full term might equal 1 PDU per month.
- Serving as an active volunteer to support a chapter BOD might equal 1 PDU one time.
- Attending a chapter presentation of 50 minutes might equal 1 PDU per month.
- Writing a newsletter article might equal 2 PDUs one time.
- Creating a new course to be accessible to the professional association might equal 5 CEUs one time.
- Writing a book on subject matter related to the occupation might equal 10 CEUs one time.
- Delivering a webinar to those outside the industry might equal 2 PDUs one time.
- Maintaining a website for the professional associations or professional organizations might equal 2 PDUs per month.
- Attending the annual international conference might equal 10 PDUs one time.
- Winning a global award associated with best practice might equal 1 CEU one time.
- Completing a 1-year project associated with the PDU might equal 20 PDUs one time.
- Getting a promotion at work, attributable to the professional certification, might equal 1 PDU one time.

Note: The key to justifying any activity as worthy of PDUs or CEUs is based on the quality of documentation. The system should allow for reasonable flexibility and promote education.

One of the identified gaps in earning PDUs pertains to understanding how alternate methods of training equate to PDUs or CEUs. In other words, it is generally accepted that a presentation of 50 minutes or longer should equal 1 PDU/CEU; however, the individual who is taking a self-paced course may have a dilemma on how to report education hours:

- **Reading printed material:** According to Stewart (2013), the average reading speed is 200–250 words per minute for nontechnical material (2 minutes per page). However, for technical content, the reading speed reduces to 50–75 words per minute, roughly 5–6 minutes per page. Let us suppose the certificant is reading a printed manual that is composed of a mix of 15 pages of nontechnical material (30 minutes) and 5–6 pages of technical content (30 minutes), for a total of 20–21 pages. Using his rule of thumb, these 20–21 pages would take 1 hour, which would equal 1 PDU/CEU.

- **Speaking/hearing printed material:** If the style for reviewing printed material is enhanced electronically by hearing someone else speak (audio) or if the person reads the content aloud, it is believed to take 1 minute per double-spaced page (or 2 minutes per single-spaced page) (Answers.com, 2010). This follows the same general rule as reading nontechnical material.

- **Viewing e-learning in a presentation format:** The average person will take approximately 3 minutes to review a presentation slide (i.e., PowerPoint). This is because the screens are primarily fixed unless they have audio, video, or animation (slide build components). Reviewing a 20-slide PowerPoint presentation could then represent 1 PDU/CEU. If there are hyperlinks on the PowerPoint slide to other content (i.e., web pages), then each additional page should include the time allotment for a web page or supplementary document.

- **Viewing a web page in a web browser:** The average person will take approximately 4 minutes to review a web page. It can take slightly longer to review content in a web page than a PowerPoint slide due to the horizontal and vertical scrolling and information being formatted differently on screen. However, if the information is streamlined, it can actually be quicker to view content on a web page. So, it could be debated that content on 20–25 web pages could take 1 hour to review, which might equate to 1 PDU/CEU.

- **Job aids:** The content on job aids should be considered technical content. Each page of a job aid should allow for 5–6 minutes per page (normal size 8.5 × 11 inches). Time allotments for blueprints or larger-size documents that expand up to 24 × 36 inches should be adjusted accordingly.

- **Visuals:** Documents that include any types of charts, diagrams, illustrations, pictures, graphs, or other forms of visualization should be considered technical content, and 5–6 minutes per page (normal size 8.5 × 11 inches) should be allowed. Time allotments for blueprints or larger-size documents that expand up to 24 × 36 inches should be adjusted accordingly.
- **Listening to sound/narration:** Audio clips have time counters, and it should be easy to convert; an audio or video is equal to 1 PDU/CEU if it is a minimum of 50 minutes.

Professional certification maintenance is critical to the ongoing success of a professional certification program. If a professional associations or professional organizations is going to be successful, it has to be clear with certificants regarding what is acceptable and how to report it. Because PDUs/CEUs are based on the honor system, it becomes central to the integrity of the individual to accurately report hours earned. On one hand, we want the system to promote sound educational practices. On the other hand, we do not want certificants to question the validity of what is acceptable to maintain professional certification.

Volunteerism

Volunteering has the tendency to bring out the good in some people. If people are not overcommitted, a professional association can grow significantly through dedicated volunteers. Being connected to a professional certification by becoming a volunteer is perhaps one of the most significant factors that will encourage the retention of a professional certification. The only factor that appears to be stronger is the commitment associated with CM. There are certain personalities and approaches that work extremely well in getting people to volunteer. These are some of the techniques that engage people to volunteer:

- Maintaining visibility on a professional association website
- Creating a sign-up calendar
- Giving small gift certificates at the end of the volunteer period
- Sending e-mails to the person's supervisor at work
- Mentioning a person's name at a professional association meeting
- Asking volunteers to recruit volunteers
- Putting volunteers on a path to join the BOD
- Publishing a newsletter and mentioning volunteers
- Giving volunteers PDUs/CEUs
- Creating levels (i.e., commended volunteer and outstanding volunteer)
- Setting time limits for volunteering (i.e., 1 month, 3 months, etc.)
- Waiving (eliminating) meeting charges for volunteers
- Having a volunteer appreciation luncheon or dinner at the end of the season

- Giving volunteers a certificate of appreciation
- Writing letters of reference for volunteers

Obtaining Lifetime Professional Certification Status

Barnhart (1997) said, "The only group capable of defining the knowledge required for a specific field may be a certifying body." Being able to obtain professional certification status for a lifetime can be valuable. It is nice to have a home paid for and a car paid for. Why not professional certification? Those applying for lifetime professional certification usually are required to meet these criteria:

- Must be in good standing up until the time of recertification
- Must have completed requirements for recertification
- Must document experience of more than 15 years of full-time professional experience (depending on the type of professional certification)
- Must complete lifetime certification application

Note: Being a member of the professional associations or professional organizations may be a plus but should not disqualify someone from lifetime membership (see definition of an illegal tying arrangement in the glossary).

The Institute for Supply Management (ISM), one of the earliest to offer professional certifications, beginning in 1915, for example offers lifetime certification. ISM states that applicants for lifetime certification should apply as soon as eligible. So, it is to the applicant's advantage not to wait because it may require additional steps and expense to realize lifetime certification status.

Conversely, according to Sears (2010), one well-known professional organization, after agreeing to lifetime membership arrangements, changed this agreement, which would have resulted in significant costs to members. Due to pressure, it became necessary to revert to the original agreement on lifetime memberships. The lesson here is to keep documentation so lifetime membership is defensible.

Reviving an Expired Professional Certification

Certifications that are offered by professional organizations usually expire more frequently than certifications offered by professional associations. Certifications from professional organizations are frequently related to information technology (IT), which changes frequently. If the professional organization did not allow the professional certification to expire, then certificants would be maintaining out-of-date professional certifications. So, allowing the professional certification to expire based on new software operating systems, for example, is usually the right decision.

Professional associations have a slightly different issue with certification expiration. Professional associations will allow a professional certification to expire, for example, 5 years from the date of issuance. This is because of a number of factors. For instance, the body of knowledge (BOK) might change significantly due to new industry knowledge. Those previously certified had knowledge that pertained to a previous BOK that has become obsolete. They are now required to understand a new BOK. Provisions may be made to have a professional certification expire and rename it to reflect a new BOK if the changes are significant. It should be noted that, in most cases, changes in a BOK can be handled through PDUs/CEUs and putting into place a supporting infrastructure that enables people to be trained on the new BOK.

Whether it is a professional organization or professional association, if there are changes to be made to the professional certification, expiration periods may be the best time to do so. For those certificants who are faced with an expiring professional certification, it can result in essentially starting all over again with the professional certification, including obtaining or verifying PDUs/CEUs. It may also mean invoicing, completing a professional certification application, retaking the professional certification exam, and paying the same cost for the certification exam as other first-time takers. professional associations or professional organizations may allow some flexibility in this process if the certificant was in good standing before the certification expired. Therefore, it is important to work closely with the professional associations or professional organizations and express the need for support.

Sunsetting a Professional Certification That Has Been Retired

Sunsetting refers to canceling a certification or allowing it to become extinct. It becomes a dead certification. A professional associations or professional organizations may decide to sunset a professional certification when:

- The perceived value of the certification has decreased due to changes in the marketplace (i.e., a job type has become obsolete due to changes in technology or process).
- The number of individuals certified is not growing despite professional association marketing efforts.
- The number of individuals certified is decreasing, which occurs when individuals fail to meet the requirements of CM (i.e., due to test/retest, recent work experience related to certification, or fees).
- The number of new applications is insufficient to justify the resources necessary to maintain the certification.
- Competition from another professional associations or professional organizations (i.e., software company) has introduced a more comprehensive or desirable professional certification program.

- Changing the requirements of the certification would be so drastic that people newly certified would be very different from those who achieved certification previously (i.e., no college degree required previously; now a college degree is required).
- The professional certification certification can no longer be supported from an infrastructure standpoint (i.e., trade journals are discontinued, chapter locations closed, merger or split of professional association governance).
- After reevaluating the professional certification, it appears that it is more appropriate to be downgraded to a certificate program.
- The certification goes through a name change, and it creates a marketing dilemma, so it is reinvented and given a new name.
- The professional associations or professional organizations is dissolved through merger, acquisition, bankruptcy, or the like.

For example, a professional certification from the HP ExpertOne website represents a good practice for professional organizations. It lists (1) certifications becoming inactive, (2) scheduled inactive date, and (3) replacement certification. It allows the viewer to show only (1) certifications becoming inactive soon, (2) inactive certifications, and (3) expired certifications. This certification website for professional organizations can be simple and efficient.

For example, those certificants who have obtained an IT professional certification must make a decision how to handle changing requirements as they arise. The different approaches are:

- Retain the inactive/expired professional certification on their résumés and hope that there will be use for it by others who have not migrated to work associated with the replacement professional certification.
- Remove the inactive/expired professional certification from their résumés once the replacement professional certification has been achieved.
- List both the inactive/expired professional certification and replacement professional certification on their résumés in hopes that it will attract prospects that have requirements for both the old and replacement professional certification.

Many certificants who sunset their professional certifications usually have no intention to use them again. However, there may be circumstances when they want to reference them:

- They want to participate on a professional associations or professional organizations BOD and provide mentoring support, and they feel their professional certification will add credibility.
- They move into a new field of consulting and feel some need to retain their designations from time to time.

■ They are completely done with working and have no intention to engage in consulting or serve on BODs.

Handling a Professional Certification That Becomes Problematic

When a professional certification becomes problematic, it is incumbent on the certificant to take action. It is not only professional association certifications that can be have problems, but also professional certification from professional organizations have challenges as well. Wyrostek (2008) discusses that IT certification also has its share of problems; he lists the top 10:

1. Certifications are vendor centric.
2. Certification's life cycle is short.
3. Certifications are not real-world oriented.
4. Certifications have been devalued.
5. There is no oversight body.
6. Degree versus certification versus experience.
7. HR people are not in touch with the real world.
8. There are budget cuts.
9. There is a glut of certified people.
10. No one knows which certifications matter.

Note: Wyrostek's article is worth reviewing because Cisco is highly regarded. As stated in the article description on Cisco's website (http://www.ciscopress.com): "Less than 10 years ago, certification was a surefire way to enter the growing IT sector. But certification no longer guarantees that you will be able to find a high quality job in IT. It still has its place, but the IT certification industry has faced some systemic problems that no one has addressed since its emergence. Warren Wyrostek calls on personal and real-world experience to share the top 10 problems with IT certification."

In addition to what Wyrostek pointed out, signs that the professional certification is becoming problematic can be noticed when these occur:
   – The professional certification becomes tainted and has a bad reputation.
   – Certification renewal fees dramatically increase and become unaffordable.
   – Membership in the professional association dramatically increases and becomes unaffordable.
   – Professional certification is dissolved by the sponsoring organization.
   – The professional certification is slated for discontinuation.
   – The amount of recertification becomes extensive to the point you cannot keep up (i.e., requiring recertification every year).

- Confusion exists or there is a real lack of clarity on the purpose of the credential.
- There is a significantly high failure rate on re-certification exam; the majority fail, and you are unable to pass the exam after multiple attempts.
- The number of people coming to meetings decreases.
- The number of people attending national conferences decreases.
- The number of people complaining increases.
- The number of people recertifying decreases.
- The number of people engaging in educational activities decreases.
- The amount of dues received by the professional association decreases.
- People stop using the designation after their name.
- People stop referencing the credential on their résumé.
- Social media (i.e., LinkedIn, Facebook, and Twitter) give the professional associations or professional organizations a bad name.
- The number of hits to the website decreases.
- The size of content in trade journals decreases.

Reinstating a Professional Certification after It Has Been Revoked

Under some circumstances, a professional certification can be revoked by a professional associations or professional organizations. Revoking a professional certification can happen any time after the application is accepted. Revoking a professional certification happens under a number of circumstances:

- The professional certification was issued by mistake (i.e., the person failed the test [scoring error]).
- The certified individual violates the code of conduct and professional ethics.
- The person is believed to have cheated on the assessment.
- The assessment questions were divulged to other parties.
- The designation was misused.
- The person has a felony conviction.
- The person is guilty of gross negligence or professional misconduct.
- There was fraud on the professional certification application (PCA).
- The certificant demonstrates unethical behavior that is reported.

All of these situations seem frightening, but they do happen, and some people have found themselves in precarious positions trying to reestablish their credentials. If a certificant is in this position, some of the questions he or she should ask include:

- Is the professional certification worth the effort of seeking reinstatement, or should I find another professional certification instead?
- Should I obtain legal support in an attempt to clear my name?
- What reinstatement policies will I be required to meet?
- What documentation do I currently have to support my claim?
- What is the normal processing time for my reinstatement application?
- How can I obtain a reinstatement application?
- How many PDUs/CEUs do I need to have to be eligible for reinstatement?

If a certificant has determined that it is worth attempting to reinstate a revoked professional certification, the certificant may find it worth considering these approaches:

- See if the professional associations or professional organizations will consider moving the revoked status to an on-hold status due to revocation being harder to address than an on-hold status.
- Find out who to speak with if there are more questions about the reinstatement of the professional certification.
- Clarify the issue of why the professional certification was revoked. If the information surrounding the revocation was incomplete or incorrect, all facts should be presented.
- Draft a letter to the legal department of the professional associations or professional organizations expressing why he or she feels it is worth considering reinstatement of the certification.
- Admit to any violation on his or her part and how he or she has changed since then.
- Request a conditional reinstatement if a full reinstatement is not possible.
- Present a letter of reference that shows improved professional behaviors.
- Create a list of projects completed so the work products are easy to review.

If the person fails in the attempt to reinstate the professional certification, the person should:

- Respect the decision of the professional associations or professional organizations not to reinstate the professional certification;
- Keep the information confidential and not communicate this revoked status;
- Remove the designation from his or her name;
- Remove any current reference to the professional certification from his or her résumé;
- Add a supplemental page to his or her résumé indicating when the credential was received and the date the use of the credential ended. It is not necessary to specify the condition by which the professional certification ended unless the professional associations or professional organizations requires this of the certificant.

Deciding Not to Maintain Professional Certification

According to research by Knapp & Associates (2007), approximately 20% of those who achieved a professional certification decided not to maintain it. Warning indicators that a certificant will stop maintaining a professional certification are represented by the following behaviors:

- Complaining about his or her level of satisfaction with the professional associations or professional organizations
- Leaving the job and pursuing a new career
- No longer using the designation on his or her name
- Not taking the required continuing education courses
- No longer being associated with the professional associations or professional organizations
- Lack of instrumental use of the professional certification
- Not approaching the professional associations or professional organizations for lifetime professional certification
- Lack of reading interest in industry trade journals

People decide not to maintain professional certification because of the following conditions:

- Retirement
- Lack of motivation
- Perception that too few people are involved in the professional certification
- Feeling that professional association meetings, conferences, and events are becoming too large
- Inability to network with other professionals
- Major career change, perhaps resulting in the professional certification becoming nontransferable
- Maintaining membership in the professional association becomes cost prohibitive
- Inability to fulfill continuing education requirements
- Identification of another professional certification that is more desirable

Suggested Reading

Answers.com. (2010). What is the average time it takes to read aloud one full page of text? Retrieved from http://wiki.answers.com/Q/What_is_the_average_time_it_takes_to_read_aloud_one_full_page_of_text.

Arbet, S., Lathrop, J., and Hooker, R., (2009). Using practice analysis to improve the certifying examinations for professional associations. *Journal of the American Academy of Physician Assistants* February. Retrieved December 11, 2012, from http://www.jaapa.com/using-practice-analysis-to-improve-the-certifying-examinations-for-pas/article/127551/.

ASAE and the Center for Association Leadership. (2006). *7 Measures of Success: What Remarkable Associations Do That Others Don't.* American Management Press.

Barnhart, P. (1997). *The Guide to National Professional Certification Programs,* 2nd ed. Boca Raton, FL: CRC Press and Amherst, MA: HRD Press.

Institute for Supply Management. (n.d.). CPM Lifetime Certification Requirements. Retrieved January 2, 2013, from http://www.ism.ws/certification/content.cfm?ItemNumber=4689.

Sears, D. (2010). CompTIA Lifetime Certification Change Creates Controversy. Retrieved January 15, 2013, from http://www.eweek.com/c/a/IT-Management/CompTIA-Lifetime-Certification-Change-Creates-Controversy-734223/.

Stewart, B. (2013). Rule of thumb (heuristic) for calculating a PDU/CEU for printed self-study material. Phone interview, January 15.

Chapter 6

Good Business Practices for Professional Certification

Key Lessons

- Defining Best Practices
- Developing the Professional Association Board of Directors
- Increasing Member Satisfaction
- Improving Communication with Professional Organizations
- Motivating Others to Become Professionally Certified
- Building a Culture that Supports Professional Certification
- Promoting a Learning Organization
- Networking for Continuous Improvement
- Weighing Certification Options
- Determining the Impact of Professional Certification Programs
- Monitoring Cash Flow Specific to Certification Maintenance
- Measuring Volunteer Engagement
- Calculating Return on Investment for Training
- Creating Training Materials for Certification Preparation

Defining Best Practices

Some people debate that the operational definition of *best practices* can have different meanings:

- The current standard, which is based on the best-known way of doing something
- One of a number of great methods that are endorsed and accepted by the industry
- Situation-specific founded on specified criteria in a particular occupation
- The preferred way of doing something based on popular opinion
- The agreed-on approach based on expert analysis of how something should be done

The goal of looking at what is good versus not good in the context of best practices is to discover what meets versus does not meet the expectations of the professional associations and professional organizations, certification solutions providers (CSPs), certificants, and accrediting agencies (i.e., National Commission for Certifying Agencies, NCCA).

When you ask the average professional associations and professional organizations about its mission and vision, many would agree they are in the business of creating and sustaining quality certification programs. So, to remain conservative in this discussion, the term *good business practices* is used. There are two factors that should be considered:

- The professional associations and professional organizations (staff and volunteers)
- The customer (certificants)
- The certification solutions providers
- Certifying agencies

Please keep in mind, by using the terminology *good business practices* I am not necessarily saying that the approach of one professional association is better than that of a professional organization. The recommended processes and approaches that professional associations and professional organizations use to implement and maintain their professional certification programs will be governed by a number of factors, such as:

- Mission and vision of the professional associations and professional organizations
- Industry focus and body of knowledge supported
- Experience with their certifications and number of different certification programs

- Collaborative relationships with other professional associations and professional organizations
- Scope (regional, national, or global) and number of certificants
- Perceived need for and pursuit of accreditation (i.e., through NCCA or American National Standards Institute [ANSI])
- Requirements for achieving certification and process for certification maintenance
- Exam preparation materials
- Strategic direction and plans
- Challenges, success, and marketplace demand the professional associations and professional organizations has experienced

When professional associations and professional organizations staff and volunteers think of good business practices, they think in terms of:

1. Customer relationship management and capability to run reports and metrics
2. Financial stability and profitability
3. Clear policies and procedures and adherence to regulations
4. Dependable information technology (IT)
5. Stable facilities and supporting infrastructure, including website presence
6. Growing staff, promotions, and employee/volunteer retention
7. Compliance with the law and conformance with accounting procedures
8. Good working relationships with the board of directors (BOD)
9. Successful collaboration with suppliers and vendors
10. Professional fulfillment that comes from seeing people become certified

When customers (certificants) think of good business practices, they envision:

1. A seamless process to apply for and obtain certification
2. Certification that has industry value
3. Proud association with a professional association and professional organization
4. Easy-to-maintain certification
5. Affordable certification preparation materials that are readily available
6. Ability to attend informative annual conferences
7. Availability of webinars and online training
8. Networking opportunities to meet other certificants
9. Receipt of trade journals or publications to stay informed
10. Making a financial investment through membership in the professional associations and professional organizations to stay connected

When certification solutions providers think of good business practices, they anticipate:

1. A certification that will have at least a 3- to 5-year life span
2. Multiple competitors developing similar certification materials
3. The need for certification exam simulation questions
4. An opportunity to present exam crash course instructor-led content
5. A possibility for creating e-learning certification maintenance course content
6. The demand for printed certification manuals
7. The requirement for flash cards (paper based or electronic)
8. The necessity to generate course certificates of completion
9. The request to help track professional development units/continuing education units (PDUs/CEUs)
10. Possible request to return outdated materials for updating/recycling

When certifying agencies think of good business practices, they expect:

1. Market research to have been performed before launching the certification
2. The professional associations and professional organizations to have obtained professional consultation from a consultant
3. A knowledgeable BOD to be established in the professional associations and professional organizations
4. Dedicated volunteers to be identified for the professional associations and professional organizations
5. Key stakeholders to be supportive of the certification
6. Financial stability to sustain the professional associations and professional organizations
7. Honesty and integrity in how testing and scoring will be performed
8. Established bylaws for supporting chapters
9. Strategic plan that includes short-term and long-term goals
10. Accredited certification programs (i.e., NCCA or ANSI)

Developing the Professional Association Board of Directors

There are a number of things that professional associations need to do to ensure they are developing the association so that it can reach its growth potential while protecting the association from a legal perspective. Some may look at this in terms of association development and risk management.

▪ **Finding the right people:** While commitment of individuals and a desire to serve is commendable, the BOD should be selective in attracting the talent that will add the most value. While serving on the board might seem interesting, not everyone can make the necessary commitment to be a board member. More important, not everyone is capable of investing the extra effort to ensure the board is as successful as it can be. The board must be conscious of the person's desire to be on the board and ensure there are no hidden agendas. Finding the right qualified candidates to serve on the board can be challenging. It comes primarily from certificants and by recycling board members. A mixture of both seems to be the optimal solution. Those board members who have served previously understand how the board should run and are in a good position to train new board members. Acquiring new board members brings in fresh ideas.

- **Developing the right people:** The Certified Association Executive (CAE) certification program offered by the American Society of Association Executives (ASAE) recognizes accepted levels of expertise in the profession with the goal of improving professional standards in association management. CAE certification requires experience and recent service as paid staff at a qualifying organization.

- **Helping the right people embrace diversity and culture:** Diversity training has been a traditional approach to developing a respect for and appreciation of different walks of life. The trend has been to continue with diversity training and incorporate multiculturalism, an awareness and understanding of other cultures, from not only a specific ethnic group or culture but also subcultures within a culture. While diversity training concerns itself with issues pertaining to gender, race, sexual preference, and the like, multiculturalism focuses on issues such as values, beliefs, traditions, customs, and the like. When constructing a BOD, having a healthy balance of male and female and different cultures can promote harmony, which sends a positive message to membership. When members notice diversity on the BOD, they may feel more socially comfortable. This being said, it may not be sensible to coerce different types of people to be on the board for the purpose of diversity. BOD involvement should be voluntary, and people with different backgrounds should feel welcome to join.

- **Retaining the right people:** People's time is valuable. Every effort should be made to express appreciation to the BOD. While the board of a professional association is not financially compensated for their efforts, there are things that can be instituted to show these individuals are valued. This might include free attendance at local chapter meetings or annual national conferences. Depending on the finances of the professional association, it may also include refreshments at BOD meetings. It is also not unreasonable to consider reimbursing expenses associated with travel on behalf of the professional association. So, if a BOD needs to visit the professional association corporate headquarters, the local chapter can expense this item. The key is to avoid circumstances where a BOD has a financial burden to serve as unpaid volunteers. The only exception may be if a BOD member provides a paid-for service (i.e., is the accountant).

Increasing Member Satisfaction

Surveys indicate that members are favorably disposed toward associations, and the negatives are minimal in general. Moreover, when someone decides no longer to be a member of an association, it is primarily due to life changes or career transitions (Dalton and Dignam, 2007). People like being association members because they can

- Develop short- or long-term relationships with people from other organizations
- Choose a level of engagement as a periodic visitor or active volunteer
- Select the programs they want to hear about from the published schedule
- Visit other association chapter meetings in different cities or countries
- Access information or services via the website
- Attach themselves to the image of the association

Many individuals may place a professional association on their list of top 10 people engagements, for example:

1. Close family
2. Friends
3. Extended family
4. Religious/political affiliation
5. Work group
6. Professional association
7. Neighbors
8. Hobby/special interest
9. Social network
10. Casual acquaintances

How a professional association addresses member value and relationships is core, common, and critical to its long-term success. Some organizations do an outstanding job at making members feel comfortable in addition to maintaining member value. Based on research (Dalton and Dignam, 2007), when members were surveyed about what they thought were the most important functions of an association, they responded as follows:

- Providing training/professional development to members
- Providing technical information or professional development to members

- Providing timely information about the field to members
- Connecting practitioners within the field to each other/networking
- Creating and disseminating standards of practice
- Representing the field to the public
- Representing the field to the government
- Representing the field within the industry or discipline
- Providing certification opportunities

What are some factors that gain member confidence?

- Maintaining a quality, up-to-date professional website
- Publishing a member-focused newsletter
- Encouraging diversity and multiculturalism in membership
- Supporting a gender-neutral environment so both men and women are represented
- Inviting the employers to participate in professional associations and professional organizations events
- Having positive visibility in the local and national media
- Receiving compliments from employers about individuals who have been certified

Improving Communication with Professional Organizations

Do professional organizations really need to be concerned about improving communication with certificants? The answer is yes. professional organizations are structured differently from professional associations, and interacting with certificants is different. Many professional organizations find it challenging to provide ongoing high-quality customer service to their certificants. This is due to the:

- Competitive nature of the industry with those who offer certification in support of their products and services (i.e., IT vendors);
- Increasing demands for just-in-time information and support that has been requested by companies for their certificants;
- Certificants' demands for certification products and services to be up to date and state of the art (i.e., e-learning accessible at anytime and from anywhere);
- Interest from certificants in communities of practice as alternative methods to provide for training and development; and
- Networking forums available to support benchmarking and best practices.

What are the basics that certificants expect from professional organizations in terms of support?

1. **Information is readily accessible:** In random searches at a number of major professional organization websites, broken links to certification content were encountered. Why is this the case?
2. **Answers to certificant's questions:** For example, VMware's certification, which as of January 2013 was rated in the top 10 IT certifications, provides comprehensive information through lists of FAQs (frequently asked questions).
3. **Contacts:** For example, CompTIA provides details about who to reach for support.
4. **Easy to navigate:** SAP's website is intuitive and easy to follow.
5. **User Friendly:** Oracle's website is welcoming in its design.

How does a professional organization communicate with certificants?

- Directly via website: frequently
- Directly via e-mail: frequently
- Directly via postal mail: periodically
- Directly via phone call from customer services: sometimes
- Indirectly via third-party organizations: periodically
- Directly person to person: rarely

What methods of communication are utilized?

- Website
- Trade journals
- In-person conferences
- Web-based conferences (video or telephone)
- Company tour

What appears to be missing in some cases for professional organizations that are not well established?

- Ability to locate key contacts regarding certification due to the size of the professional organization
- Access to individuals who can support career counseling
- Access to local chapters
- Communities of practice
- Annual conferences
- Newsletters or trade journals
- Personalized customer service

Motivating Others to Become Professionally Certified

The following are some random excerpts from certification programs extracted verbatim from their websites (retrieved January 17, 2013). As I searched the Internet for certifications using keyword searches, different ones appeared. To attract certificants, certification descriptions should be engaging, as these appear to be. I did not evaluate these certifications, and these are not endorsed.

- **Certified Regulatory Compliance Manager (CRCM):** Is designed to establish a recognized standard of knowledge and competence for regulatory compliance professionals working in the financial services industry, formally recognize those who meet these standards, provide employers with a tool to identify skilled, knowledgeable professionals, and support the benefits of professional continuing education and development.
- **Certified Fraud Examiner (CFE):** Position yourself at the forefront of your profession by becoming a Certified Fraud Examiner (CFE). Denoting proven expertise in fraud prevention and detection, the CFE credential is recognized in the hiring and promotion policies of leading organizations around the world.
- **Certified Mortgage Banker (CMB):** Designation is the industry standard of professional success. It symbolizes respect, credibility, ethics, and achievement within real estate finance. Earning a CMB instantly places you at the top of our dynamic industry and makes you a part of the elite group that has achieved the highest level of professional success.
- **Certified Interior Decorators International (C.I.D.):** Is dedicated to individuals who have the talent and seek educational training and the required testing to become recognized as "Certified" professionals in the interior decorating industry.
- **Certified Rehabilitation Counselor (CRC):** Must demonstrate that they are of good moral character, meet acceptable standards of quality in their practice, and have the requisite education and professional background. To become certified, rehabilitation counselors must meet stringent eligibility requirements including advanced education and work experience, and must achieve a passing score on the CRC Exam.
- **Certified Franchise Executives (ICFE):** The mission of the Institute is to enhance the professionalism of franchising by certifying the highest standards of quality training and education. The ICFE offers a wide range of continuing education programs for professional development. Meeting the requirements of the program and completing the course of study leads to the Certified Franchise Executive (CFE) designation.
- **Certified Protection Professional:** A CPP designation represents the pinnacle of achievement in the private security field. The designation requires the candidate to meet or exceed very high standards and pre-requisites including, a certain level of years and background in the security industry, multiple

references, and the ability to pass an extremely grueling four-hour certification test that assesses the candidate's knowledge of all aspects of physical, intellectual, and personnel security.

■ **Certified Hospitality Educator:** The award-winning CHE program, the only professional development opportunity designed for hospitality educators around the world, enables you to strengthen students' critical thinking and motivation to learn, share ideas with your peers, and receive recognition for your teaching abilities from students, colleagues, and the industry.

■ **Certified Travel Counselor (CTC):** Program teaches owners and managers how to analyze new business opportunities, develop marketing strategies, and negotiate.

Building a Culture That Supports Professional Certification

What is culture, and why is it important? Culture is the collective behaviors, values, beliefs, norms, language, habits, systems, and symbols. It influences the way people interact with each other inside the culture and has an impact on how they choose to engage with external individuals who come into contact with the culture. An organization's culture may contain subcultures, which may be due to location, size, tenure of employees, personality characteristics of people at that location, and so on. Cultural independence allows different attitudes and ways of thinking to coexist.

Organizational culture affects the way people feel and if strengthened can result in an ethical workplace that fosters respect, integrity, and good working relationships. Strengthening an organizational culture is an ongoing process that requires training, organizational development, and related processes, of which professional certification is a part. Change management as it relates to an organization occurs over time and may be the result of changing management or leadership.

To build a culture that supports professional certification, these types of questions should be answered:

■ Why does culture change need to occur to support professional certification programs?
■ What are the most effective ways to build a culture that will sustain professional certification long term?
■ Who do we need to inspire people to go above and beyond?
■ When should we motivate people who have expressed no interest in professional certification programs?
■ Where can we create an inclusive environment to engage all employees?

- How do we extend ourselves so that we have a global reach?
- Which professional certification programs will be of greatest value to the most people?

Promoting a Learning Organization

A *learning organization* is a company that facilitates the learning of its employees and continuously transforms itself to remain up to date. Peter Senge's 1994 book *The Fifth Discipline* popularized the idea of the learning organization. In 1997, the *Harvard Business Review* identified Senge's text as one of the seminal management books of the past 75 years. Peter Senge asserts that individual learning is a prerequisite for organizational learning to occur.

Building the learning organization involves creating a climate for continuous learning. One of the ways to create these atmospheric conditions is to make learning a habit (Marquardt, 1996). professional certification makes ongoing learning an objective through certification maintenance requirements. If learning is engaging, it can become addictive. Engaging learning requires using blended training approaches, such as:

- Instructor-led training
- Conferences
- E-learning
- Experiential activities, such as shadowing

How can you take the temperature of employees to find out if they are "well" or "sick" of training?

- Conduct surveys to determine their level of satisfaction with the training
- Give people assessments to see what they have learned
- Observe the workplace to see if training has been used
- See what effect the training is having on the organization's processes
- Calculate the return on investment or return on quality of the training

By redefining learning and making it part of the daily schedule, the organization can look forward to training experiences, for example:

- Introduce quarterly coffee-and-donut breakfasts where lessons learned can be shared
- Implement monthly brown bag lunch-and-learn events where employees bring their own meal
- Create annual appreciation dinners where a guest speaker delivers a key topic

- Launch weekly huddles in different departments where people share key learning
- Consider taking a tour of another company twice a year to see how other companies do things

Training and development need a different look from time to time if people will be receptive to learning new things. The whole organization needs to take part in this process. People may be averse to being trained but like the idea of learning new things. Metaphorically speaking,

- The training and development function needs a thermostat so it can determine if those in the organization are learning and how much they are learning. A needs assessment is a type of thermostat that can be used to determine people's receptivity to learning.
- Sales and marketing may utilize a climate control function to adjust to changing circumstances. Sometimes, climate control will be on autopilot when sales and marketing is working and then should be switched to manual when training is needed.
- The human resources department needs to understand and create awareness of the organization's forecast, which represents the tactical and strategic plans and direction.
- The operations department needs to be in tune with the weather. Weather represents the sociopolitical elements of what is going on in the organization (i.e., culture change initiatives such as mergers and acquisitions). In good weather, training can be turned up, and in bad weather, training may need to be turned up even more.

Networking for Continuous Improvement

Networking for continuous improvement is particularly important for certification professionals. The options include:

- Working with the professional associations and professional organizations to identify opportunities the professional associations and professional organizations has for networking:
  - Professional organizations have a tendency to network within their own product and service offerings due to the competitive nature of the certifications.
  - Professional associations are sometimes willing to have a joint meeting between two different associations that complement each other, such as project management and supply chain management, finance and accounting, or human resources and training.

- Collaborating with other certification networking associations, such as
  - The Certification Network Group (CNG), which was started by Judy Rosenbloom in the early 1980s, works with other groups such as ICE and holds meetings periodically throughout the year, primarily in the Washington, D.C., area.
  - ASAE provides large conferences and virtual communities to support communication.
- Social media
  - LinkedIn
  - Twitter
- Facebook

While networking and accessing social media are great ideas, safety and security should also be kept in mind. There is increased sensitivity due to the Safe Harbor Act of 1998 and identity theft issues that continue to occur as the result of computer hackers. If posting credentials on websites, it is good to periodically search the name to ensure it is not showing up in strange places.

Weighing Certification Options

Weighing different certification options involves looking at what will give the individual and organization the greatest value. Assigning weights to certification options looks at specific criteria. A weighting system is a method for quantifying qualitative data to minimize the effect of bias. Most systems involve:

- Assigning a numerical weight to each of the evaluation criteria
- Rating the prospective sellers in each criterion
- Multiplying the weight by the rating
- Totaling the resultant products to compare an overall score
- Optionally, creating a legend is optional, which is preferred for final presentation

As demonstrated in the following example, those involved in the evaluation process gather all responses and place them in the grid referencing an identification number. A legend can be used at the bottom to indicate what the legend represents. As can be seen in Table 6.1, project management certification is the most preferred, followed by training and development. It is followed closely by quality assurance, which is also important to note.

Table 6.1 Weighing Certification Options

Evaluation Criteria	A	B	C	W	A	B	C
Number of people requesting certification	5	3	4	5	25	15	20
Number of hours to complete certification	4	5	4	4	16	20	16
Cost of certification	4	4	4	3	12	12	12
					53	47	48

A, project management; B, quality assurance; C, training and development.

Determining the Impact of Professional Certification Programs

It is important to be in agreement on the definition of impact analysis before performing one. An impact analysis can mean several things, and there are different perspectives on how to conduct an impact analysis. For example, some think of an impact analysis as:

- The evaluation of the positives and negatives of pursuing a particular course of action in light of its possible risks (uncertainties) or the extent and nature of change it may cause
- The effect that a course of action had on the business (i.e., people becoming certified)
- The result of the change to policies, processes, and procedures

When one looks at conducting an impact analysis as it applies to certification, they can:

- Look at the effect certification had on improving performance
- Review the cycle time certified individuals had on increasing productivity
- Observe the enhancements that resulted through integration, harmonization, or standardization that can be tied to certification
- View the logs, records, and reports to identify trends and develop forecasts using best practices. The act of certification here may simply be improved metrics

The following key considerations should be kept in mind regarding an impact analysis:

1. An impact analysis can only be correct when the criteria are defined up front.
2. A decision must be made about what to measure before you can measure it.
3. Determine how to measure the item in question.
4. Measurement must be made, preferably in more than one way.
5. The measurement should be confirmed and verified.

Monitoring Cash Flow

Companies such as Microsoft and Cisco (classified as professional organizations) have done an excellent job at maintaining certification value. They have:

- Certified millions of people and maintain a large pipeline of new applicants
- Mastered the art of maintaining high-quality educational products and services
- Money, which enables them to retain the necessary staff to support certification

On the other hand, some professional associations have the opposite set of circumstances. They are:

- Established as a nonprofit or not-for-profit entity
- Challenged with generating revenue and maintaining financial stability
- Required to carefully monitor cash flow to ensure long-term survival

Professional associations, especially at the chapter level, can become vulnerable to financial collapse due to the significant competition for members who will pay for their services. Therefore, they need to have a plan that will help them creatively generate revenue:

- Implement professional development days to sell PDUs/CEUs
- Set up dinner meetings with a speaker and charge for each seat
- Coordinate study groups and supporting materials and charge each participant
- Pursue sponsorships from major companies
- Ask for donations from members
- Request contributions from recruiters who obtain employee referrals from the professional association
- Sell advertising space in newsletters and on the professional association website
- Charge vendors for a presentation table at chapter meetings and events

Measuring Volunteer Engagement Specific to Certification Maintenance

Volunteers are an essential ingredient to the success of a professional association. They can earn PDUs/CEUs for their effort. The level to which volunteers can be engaged can be looked at as:

- **Certification application review:** The number of hours a volunteer invests in administrative tasks related to helping a certificant obtain/maintain certification. Use $50 per hour for this equation. The certification maintenance task may involve looking at a renewal application that contains work history since the individual was last certified (i.e., 3 to 5 years ago). If the process of reviewing the recertification application (certification renewal) takes 10 hours, then the value of the volunteer effort is worth $500. This figure represents true net value because it is nontaxable, and the individual is not compensated for his or her effort. If the professional associations and professional organizations has 250 applications that are recertified per year, then the value of the volunteer effort is 2,500 hours or $125,000 per year.

- **PDU/CEU data entry:** If a professional associations and professional organizations does not have an automated system for maintaining PDU/CEU information, it will need to manually track PDUs/EUs. This can be a daunting task because each certificant may be engaging in different activities to maintain PDUs/CEUs using different solutions providers. If an online database is constructed, the professional associations and professional organizations still needs to have someone assigned who will review (audit) the entries to ensure accuracy. The value for data entry should be computed at $50 per hour, and the value of auditing should be computed at $50 per hour. Ideally, the person who is entering PDUs/CEUs should be a different individual from the person who is performing the audit. If the auditing process is subject to errors, then a second checker should be assigned to the process. Second checks are essential if the certification is associated with any compliance-related position. The credibility of the professional associations and professional organizations could be at stake if recording is not accurate.

- **Identifying opportunities/locating solutions providers for PDUs/CEUs:** Researching people, places, and vendors who can provide PDU/CEU options and then making this information available to certificants is significantly beneficial. The research effort is worth $50 per hour. If 200 hours can be invested each year in coming up with renewed options for earning PDUs/CEUs, the volunteer value is $10,000.

- **Volunteers creating and delivering PDUs/CEUs as the solutions provider:** When volunteers design or develop deliverables that are worthy of PDUs/CEUs (i.e., presentations to the chapter, e-learning programs, etc.), it is of significant value to the certificant. The average cost of 1 PDU/CEU will range from $25 to $100, depending on the content. It is common for a professional associations and professional organizations to require 20 PDUs/CEUs more or less per year to maintain certification. If $50 is used for the average cost of a PDU/CEU, then $1,000 per year is the investment each certificant is expected to make to maintain certification. Where does the average person get the $1,000? Some of them get it from their company, others pay for it themselves, and many focus on opportunities where they can get the PDU without paying for it. Even though the person did not pay for the PDU/CEU in some instances, it should still be calculated to have value. The time to develop a quality 1-hour presentation is 20 hours. If $50 per hour is used for this computation, then the value of 1 PDU/CEU that is created by a volunteer is $1,000. If you can have 20 volunteers create 20 courses, then the value is $20,000.

- **Volunteers negotiating savings:** There are some instances when volunteers (i.e., board members) are able to obtain speakers at no charge (or reduced charge less travel expenses). This value should be $1,000 per 1-hour presentation, which equals 1 PDU/CEU. Using senior leaders from local companies has become a preferable speaker option.

- **Website management:** Having someone design and maintain the professional association website can be of substantial value. Large-scale websites may be impractical to manage with a part-time web developer. A large-scale website is represented by a full-time, 30- to 40-hour-per-week job. However, a small-to-medium size website that has static content that does not change may be easy to manage once it is set up. It might take 1 to 5 hours per week or up to 20–30 hours per month. This could be managed by one or more volunteers. If a website takes 20 hours per month to manage and the average value of $50 per hour is associated with this task, then the volunteer value is $1,000 per month.

- **Newsletter/communication:** Creating newsletters, chapter meeting flyers, brochures, and other related messages can be a time-consuming task. These can take 10–20 hours per month for a small-to-medium size professional association. If $50 per hour is used for the calculation, then $1,000 is the realized value of this volunteer effort.

- **Sales and marketing:** professional associations will sometimes create products or services to sell to certificants or prospective certificants to generate revenue. For example, sometimes there is a participation fee for joining a certification study group, or there may be a cost for certification study materials created by the professional association. Another example could involve a professional development day, which is a method for a professional association to generate revenue by bringing in multiple speakers to present topics so certificants can earn PDUs/CEUs. If volunteers are serving as sales and marketing people, then the value of their volunteer effort is represented by the sales that are generated for the professional association.

Table 6.2 Calculating the Value of Volunteer Contributions

Volunteer	Category	Number of Hours	Hourly Value	Total Value
John	Application review	4	25	100
Sally	PDU/CEU data entry	10	20	200
Rick	Solution providers	2	50	100
Pat	Negotiations	2	40	80
Mike	Website	3	60	180
Jean	Newsletter/ communications	12	20	240
Joe	Sales and marketing	5	30	150
Mary	General administration	15	20	300
Pete	Use of facilities	2	200	400

- **General administration:** Serving as a key point of contact for the professional association by handling inquiries and responding to communications has the value of a secretarial assistant. This value could be estimated at $25 per hour.
- **Use of facilities:** When meetings or special presentations are required, some certificants who are members of large companies may have access to auditoriums. Renting facilities can be quite expensive, in the hundreds or even thousands of dollars. As part of sponsoring the event, the company may even provide refreshments.

These categories are general, and there may be others that are more fitting to a professional associations and professional organizations. The importance of tracking volunteer efforts is that they can be looked at as contributions. Keeping a record of these contributions is valuable for auditing purposes as well as strategic planning. For example, the free auditorium that was available last year might not be available next year. Most of these examples apply to professional associations, but there could be some examples for which a professional organization has an established relationship with a volunteer organization that supports its certification program. Table 6.2 can be used to track and calculate volunteer efforts.

Calculating Return on Investment (ROI) for training and Certification programs can be performed in a number of ways. Some important considerations when considering what method to use, may be in part influenced by these factors:

- Payback periods
- Opportunity costs for choosing one training initiative over another

- Sunk costs – dollars invested in technology, i.e., learning management systems used to deliver training
- Break-even point where recouping the value of training can be realized
- Etc.

It is recommended to consider both quantitative and qualitative methods for calculating training ROI. While an increase in productivity might be a quantitative measure, increases in employee morale might be a valuable qualitative measure. Some methods such as Return on Quality (ROQ) could be looked at as a subset of ROI depending upon the context. If training reinforces compliance and supports quality initiatives, then it can potentially be looked at from a financially beneficial perspective.

There are a number of very good authors who hold workshops specifically on measuring training ROI such as Knowledge Advisors and Jack Phillips. The simplest and most practical part of the equation should address:

- ROI = Realized Tangible Benefits – Costs Incurred
- Ideally if it can be determined, review the financial and non-financial costs
- Investment can be looked at from a monetary and non-monetary perspective
- Each environment is situation specific for measuring ROI
- Manufacturing or production environments can result in significant ROI for training
- Community service initiatives can have a large training ROI that is hard to calculate
- ROI factors should be defined upfront and be reviewed periodically to gauge performance
- Define what should be measured
- Keep the variables well defined and categorized
- Looking at training ROI for learning and development projects may be more straight forward to calculate than training initiatives that are association with ongoing operations

Calculating the ROI for certification could include the factors associated with training and the value of the certification. Value includes items such as:

- Regulatory requirements
- Compliance mandates
- Perceived worth to stakeholders (internal and external)
- Impacts to products and service quality
- Benefits of keeping the certificant up to date by requiring certification maintenance through ongoing education

Calculating Return on Investment for Training (an Example Model)

Human Capital ROI Model Focused on Performance Improvement (PI)	
Training and certification cost per participant	$ 1,000
Average fully loaded salary of participant	$50,000
*Estimated PI, including training	30%
**Isolated PI due to training	60% of the 30% above
Isolated PI relative to time spent performing skills on the job	20%
Adjustment for bias, confidence, conservatism	65%
Training impact on PI adjusted for bias	30% × 60% × 20% × 65% = 2.34%
Calculate monetized benefit	$50,000 × 2.34% = $1,170
Calculate ROI	$1,170 - $1,000 = $170
Calculate benefit-to-cost ratio	$1,170/$1,000 = $1.17
This could also be interpreted as a 17% improvement.	

*This methodology was created by Knowledge Advisors. It is a conservative approach to calculating training ROI.

To determine the measurement, requests need to be formulated like the following or similarly:

- Given all factors, including certification, estimate how much your job performance related to the course subject matter will improve. *Please indicate from 0% to 100%.*
- Based on the prior question, estimate how much of the improvement will be a direct result of this certification. (For example, if you feel that half of your improvement is a direct result of the training, indicate 50% here.) *Please indicate from 0% to 100%.*
- What percentage of total work time requires knowledge and skills presented in this certification? *Please indicate from 0% to 100%.*

Evaluating professional certification can also be done quantitatively or qualitatively. Basic metrics can be straightforward. However, more complex models for evaluation should use a reference and existing models.

For quantitative evaluations the focus may be the number of people certified and the financial performance of the business. For example, Hale (2002, p. 258) illustrates how to use a scatter diagram to show the correlation.

Qualitative approaches to evaluation for professional certification might propose to determine the individual impacts that certification has for individuals. For example, Brinkerhoff (2006) uses the success case method for discovery of the factors that make or break training success.

Lessons learned are an outcome of the evaluation process. Lessons learned also serve as an input into future initiatives that pertain to certification programs that need to be ranked, rated, or graded. Whether the approach is quantitative or qualitative (or a mixed method), lessons learned are essential. Lessons learned should be captured in a diary when key experiences are realized. What we propose to know regarding certification programs is what went right, what went wrong, and what could have been done differently with respect to:

- Quality of the certifications and how they improved efficiencies or effectiveness
- Value certification had for a designated occupation
- Importance of certifications as they relate to strengthening the company's mission

How do you go about ranking, rating, or grading professional certification programs? Is it really necessary?

As evaluation is conducted on professional certification, there may be some challenging decisions regarding comparing which one to pursue if several claim to produce similar results for the certificant. Three classical approaches to measurement that can work for professional certification programs are:

- **Ranking:** Places the professional certification contenders on a continuum, for instance, first, second, and third. This relative approach can be misleading if first place fails to meet quality expectations.
- **Rating:** Uses classifications such as unacceptable, poor, fair, good, and excellent. Unacceptable (or poor) is an important range to include if there is a level of performance that represents the minimum standard not being met.
- **Grading:** Provides fives indicators of performance as letter grades (i.e., A, B, C, D, or F) for the performance of the professional certification. This classification may be the most accurate because each professional certification can be evaluated individually without comparison. Under a grading concept, more than one professional certification can receive a letter grade of A.

■ **Banding:** This can actually be considered as a category of grading. It provides for 15 in-between letter grades (i.e., A+, A, A-, B+, B, B-, C+, C, C-, D+, D, D-, F+, F, and F-. Banding is the most accurate concept to use. An A+ may represent a professional certification greatly exceeding expectations. An F- may represent the professional certification not only greatly failing to meet expectations but also presenting extreme risks associated with certifying people under this professional certification.

As a general rule, it is not recommended to pursue a professional certification that does not:

■ Rank first or second,
■ Rate excellent or good, or
■ Receive a grade of at least B or higher.

Tittel (2003) uses a criteria-based approach to rank certifications. The benefits of a criteria-based approach are that it enables the individual and employer to determine the values important to them. Here are some characteristics of a criteria-based approach:

■ Career level
■ Average time to completion
■ Number of exams
■ Cost of exams
■ Experience requirement
■ Income potential

Another factor that tends to influence how people think about professional certification is the ratings. Ratings come from a variety of sources, for example:

■ Job boards: emphasize employers who list the certification as a plus
■ professional associations and professional organizations: feature the certification as key to career survival
■ Trade journals: highlight the certification as great
■ Industry indices: serve as critics and compare and contrast certification popularity
■ Book authors: focus on how to maximize the instrumental use of the certification

Bad certification ratings come as the result of using improper wording, which some certifications actually have on their websites. In an effort to attract people to the certification, they make it appear effortless to obtain the certification, as can be seen by these examples:

■ Training is not necessary to become certified.

■ It is important to note that there are no eligibility requirements to become certified.

Creating Training Materials for Certification Preparation

There are some certification training materials that go a long way to help people prepare for certification exams:

1. **Certification textbooks:** These are the primary references published by the professional associations and professional organizations or supporting authors that serve as the foundation for the certification.
   a. Required texts: These are mandated by the professional associations and professional organizations.
   b. Recommended texts: These provide additional clarification.
   c. Other texts: These are mentioned by other providers as having value.
2. **Sample exam preparation questions:** The simulated exam must not use exact questions that have appeared before on any certification exam. This would constitute cheating and would subject the authors to severe penalties, including losing certification. Many professional associations and professional organizationss will publish similar questions to help people understand the structure and types of questions. To create sample test questions, there are several options:
   a. Slides in Microsoft PowerPoint
   b. Flip-books in programs such as Articulate
   c. MS Word business card templates for printing on both sides
   d. Web page services such as brainflips.com
3. **Slides:** These are used for presentation purposes (i.e., PowerPoint) and are preferred because they are easy to project.
   a. The use of color, graphics, and logically grouping information into smaller amounts (referred to as chunking) is important for instruction.
   b. Slides can be output to websites, computers, tablets, and mobile phones.
   c. Slides can incorporate different forms of media, animation, sound, and video.
4. **Posters:** Many of the process maps, flowcharts, illustrations, and diagrams are best presented using large posters.
   a. Posters can be expensive to create, especially if they are in color. It may be preferable to purchase posters that are already designed.
   b. If posters are to be created, they should be laminated and adhered to poster board so they can reused. Posters should be printed in a minimal

quantity. Each time the body of knowledge changes, the posters will need to be re-created.

5. **Flash cards:** There are many uses for flash cards; these have a concept (or question) on one side of the card and the answer (or solution) on the flip side of the card. Flash cards can be electronic or paper based. They can be large or small.
   a. Role plays
   b. Scenarios (i.e., "what if" situations)
   c. Exam questions
   d. Games

6. **Training aids:** Visual resources streamline or summarize content in a simpler form.
   a. Procedures
   b. Checklists
   c. Flowcharts
   d. Logic models
   e. Value stream maps
   f. Fishbone diagrams
   g. Decision trees
   h. Process maps

7. **Audio CDs:** These support narration of key concepts.
   a. Good for examination questions
   b. Good for terms and definitions
   c. Good for storytelling
   d. Allow for a listen-only mode of training (i.e., late at night when going to bed and eyes are tired) or meditation forms of learning

8. **Video:** Video can be used in a variety of ways to supplement learning. To accompany video, pictures, graphics, narration, music, and animation can also be incorporated.
   a. Case studies
   b. Example situations
   c. Related research

9. **Participant guides:** These are workbooks that are consistent with the instructor guide.
   a. Elaborate in sufficient detail the content covered by the instructor
   b. Supplement the primary texts used for certification

10. **Simulations:** These involve real-life experimentation or demonstration that represents on-the-job training. For example:
    a. Cardio Pulmonary Recussitaton (CPR) Dummy to demonstrate proper method of reviving a non-breathing person (or animal)
    b. Performing test methods by a laboratory technician
    c. Demonstrating appropriate counseling techniques by having a new advisor participate in a role play

    d. Construction by having the apprentice service a piece of equipment after viewing a video or reading a manual

11. **Learning games:** Interactive activities incorporate enjoyment as a basis for knowledge transfer.

    a. Board games

    b. Geocaching

    c. Ropes (Outward Bound)

    d. Team challenges

Suggested Reading

American Society of Association Executives. (2011). AMC Accreditation. Retrieved February 10, 2013, from http://www.asaecenter.org/AboutUs/contentCAE.cfm?ItemNumber=16089.

Bogan, C., and English, M. (1994). *Benchmarking for Best Practices: Winning through Innovative Adaptation.* New York: McGraw Hill.

Camp, R. (1995). *Business Process Benchmarking: Finding and Implementing Best Practices.* Milwaukee, WI: ASQ Quality Press.

Dalton, J., and Dignam, M. (2007). *The Decision to Join: How Individuals Determine Value and Why They Choose to Belong.* Washington, DC: ASAE and the Center for Association Leadership.

Damelio, R. (1995). *The Basics of Benchmarking.* Portland, OR: Productivity Press.

Hale, J. (2002). *Performance-based evaluation: Tools and techniques to measure the impact of training.* San Francisco: Jossey-Bass Pfeiffer.

Kaminski, K., and Lopes, T. (2009). *Return on investment: Training and development.* Society for Human Resource Management Academic Initiatives. Alexandria, VA: Society for Human Resource Management.

Knapp, J., Anderson, L., and Wild, C. (2009). *Certification: The ICE Handbook*, 2nd ed. Washington, DC: Institute for Credentialing Excellence.

Knowledge Advisors. (n.d.). Learning analytics workshop. Chicago: Knowledge Advisors.

Marquardt, M. (1996). *Building the Learning Organization.* New York: McGraw Hill.

Phillips, J., and Phillips, P. (2007). *Show Me the Money: How to Determine ROI in People, Projects and Programs.* San Francisco: Berrett-Koehler.

Senge, P. (1994). *The Fifth Discipline Fieldbook: Strategies and Tools for Building a Learning Organization.* New York: Crown Business.

Chapter 7

Maintaining Compliance with Professional Certification

Key Lessons

- A Reality Check
- Reinforcing a Compliance Mindset
- Enabling Feedback Mechanisms to Eliminate Blind Spots
- Auditing Professional Certification
- Evaluating Professional Certification
- Implementing a Tracking System for PDUs/CEUs
- Assigning the Job Role to Oversee Professional Certification
- Reviewing Implementability Concerns
- Sustaining Accreditation with a Recognized Authority
- Adhering to Sound Instructional Design and Curriculum Development

A Reality Check

Regulatory auditors: Knock, knock, knock!
Receptionist: Hello. May I help you?
Regulatory auditors: We would like to come in and conduct a site visit.
Site lead: I got here as soon as I could. Who would you like to speak with?

Regulatory auditors: We will be speaking with several groups today, and we are not sure yet.

Site lead: OK. I will contact the director of human resources to notify of your visit.

Director of human resources: I dropped everything to get here. What can I do for you?

Regulatory auditors: OK. We are here to conduct reviews. Could you print an organization chart and let the training department know we need training records and job descriptions.

Director of human resources: OK. We are happy to comply; you will find that our employees are highly qualified to perform their work and are up to date in their certifications.

Reinforcing a Compliance Mindset

If a person were in the opening scenario with an auditor showing up unannounced, the person might desire to have achieved related certification. For example, there are Certified Information Systems Auditor (CISA) and Compliance and Ethics Professional (CCEP) certifications that pertain to audit readiness and preapproval inspection. These particular certifications are targeted at helping professionals prepare to deal with auditors.

One certificant shared an experience with the certification in a 2013 white paper, *Five Tips to Get IT Auditors Off Your Back*. According to Grettenberger, CISA, CCEP, there are five ways to convince auditors that information technology (IT) systems conform to requirements:

1. Adopting a proactive mindset to see the big picture
2. Familiarizing oneself with what IT auditors want to see
3. Collecting evidence using automation and daily report delivery
4. Avoiding providing too much information
5. Using self-service capabilities when it makes sense

The CISA certification from the Information Systems Audit and Control Association (ISACA) and the CCEP certification from the Compliance Certification Board (CCB) represent established certification. However, the question that must be answered for those periodically dealing with auditors is, "For my industry, what certifications will prepare me for audits and enhance my credibility?" The answer to this question will undoubtedly require a historical review of the questions that have been asked previously. Most likely, this information will be available in audit files and should be available from competitors who make it available in communities of practice.

Audit readiness encourages people to become certified. Moreover, there are a significant number of people who pursue professional certification because it (1)

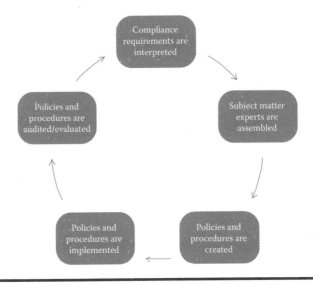

Figure 7.1   Typical process for policies and procedures.

promotes conformance with policies and procedures, (2) thereby promoting compliance with regulatory authorities. Some people are inclined to say that professional certification supports adherence to regulations, and they are correct, but it should be thought of in terms of steps or a process as illustrated in Figure 7.1.

When an organization sets out to establish policies and procedures, there are different levels of priority for maintaining compliance. Here are some examples:

- **High priority:** Regulatory authorities come in and have observations that things must change (i.e., due to safety concerns) and issue warning letters or consent decrees.
- **Medium priority:** Other agencies (local, state, and federal) have recommendations for how to improve processes or make something more efficient.
- **Low priority:** Consumers of products/services express a desire for continuous improvement in features or functions (not compliance related).

Let us take a look at a high-priority example in which professional certification can have significant value. Mature (larger and experienced) organizations are usually in a good position to correctly interpret the updated regulations. They will assign a staff person. However, a smaller startup business may be at a disadvantage because it may not have a dedicated staff person or track record with regulatory agencies. Hence, its interpretation of the regulations may be fair to good. However, if the staff at company X is small, but employees are certified (i.e., through the American Society for Quality [ASQ]), they be more invested in the quality policies and procedures development.

What does more invested mean? The term *more invested* indicates that the person has demonstrated willingness to spend the necessary time and effort to pursue certification related to his or her occupation. Through the process of professional certification through ASQ (i.e., to reach Certified Quality Auditor [CQA] professional certification), the person is required to understand the standards and principles of auditing and elements of a quality system. The CQA analyzes elements of a quality system and determines adherence to specified criteria. While it may not be fair to say the certified person is smarter, it is reasonable to state the person might be more knowledgeable. Knowledge coupled with willingness to embrace professional certification can make all the difference in how a person performs on the job. Attributes of an individual who has successfully achieved professional certification in these circumstances may result in:

- Clearer demonstrated expertise to address the procedural issues at hand
- Higher level of self-motivation to perform additional research on a policy
- More competitive spirit to succeed when questions on procedures arise
- Pride in one's work to validate the professional certification actually works and is instrumental
- Credibility with the regulatory agency that is familiar with the certification
- Access to networking forums to support procedure solutions development

Enabling Feedback Mechanisms to Eliminate Blind Spots

A feedback mechanism is a process or place that people can use to provide input, such as:

- Web survey link
- Voice mailbox
- Central e-mail address

The purpose of enabling feedback is so that communication flows between the professional associations or professional organizations and certificants as well as supporting association management companies (AMCs), business partners, accrediting agencies, and the like. When there are blind spots, individuals at the various agencies are unaware of communication gaps, which may result in disgruntled relationships. The most common form of feedback is the survey due to convenience in administering the instrument. What do people do when they get those surveys regarding satisfaction with customer service? They can:

- Respond right away honestly or falsely

- Respond later honestly or falsely
- Not respond at all

If the survey data are inaccurate, then there will be a blind spot. That said, there are a number of things that professional associations or professional organizations can do to encourage honest and timely responses:

- Put the names of those who respond in a drawing for a chance to receive a prize
- Give those who respond a discount on a product or service
- Let respondents know their comments are taken seriously and will be acted on
- Call the respondent instead of sending a computer e-mail
- Have multiple response types: e-mail, phone call, and letter

Auditing Professional Certification

Auditing professional certification includes a systematic examination of records related to the certification to check for its accuracy. The tools we use to conduct an audit might include:

- Certification checklist
- Certification certificate with updated seal as appropriate
- Transcript of professional development units/continuing education units (PDUs/CEUs)
- Demonstrated work products listed as projects

Auditing is important because it:

- Validates the individual has passed a certification exam
- Verifies the professional certification is current and the professional associations or professional organizations exists
- Ensures the person is in good standing with the certifying professional associations or professional organizations
- Confirms the person has the required number of PDUs/CEUs
- Protects the organization who represents credentials to others

Who can conduct the audit in addition to the certificant's supervisor?

- Human resources (HR)/operations
- Organizational development/training and development
- Quality assurance/quality control

When should an audit be conducted?

- Before any compliance or regulatory audit
- During the certificant's annual performance evaluation

Evaluating Professional Certification

Evaluation is the determination of merit (quality), worth (value), or significance (importance). The key to effectively and efficiently evaluate professional certification is to determine the criteria and then the approach. Criteria might include things such as:

- **The amount of financial investment:** Values could be in terms of actual cash, time allowed off during work hours, or similar things that represent all calculated costs of certification.
- **The number of people who experienced increased job satisfaction:** Satisfaction and dissatisfaction must be defined, as must the degree satisfaction has been realized.
- **The number of people who experienced increased job responsibilities:** This might require practice analysis to distinguish how the certificant is more competent to perform complex work.

The approach concerns what types of evaluation are involved. When we want to evaluate certification, depending on the circumstances and nature of what is being evaluated, we can do this through different types of lenses (perspectives), such as:

- Proposal evaluation: vendors, quotes, bids
- Product evaluation: certification materials
- Performance evaluation: realized productivity before and after certification
- Personnel evaluation: change in roles, responsibilities, and competencies
- Process evaluation: the way in which certification is pursued, completed, and maintained
- Policy evaluation: requirements for obtaining and maintaining certification
- Project evaluation: the life cycle of certification conceptualization through closure
- Program evaluation: the ongoing administration of certification programs

On the flip side, there are some who are convinced that evaluating professional certification can be performed in a simplistic fashion by looking at certification as a training initiative. Sometimes this works well, and at other times, alternative approaches, such as mentioned previously, are worth considering.

If we look at certification as a training initiative, one way in which we have traditionally evaluated training programs is using the Kirkpatrick four-level model:

- Level 1: A satisfaction survey is distributed to find out if participants liked the training.
- Level 2: An assessment is used to determine if participants learned anything from the training.
- Level 3: Behavior is observed to uncover if participants used the training.
- Level 4: Results are reviewed to see if the training had an effect.

Some have desired to take it one step further and utilize the Phillips model:

- Calculate return on investment (ROI).

If the Kirkpatrick model is applied to certification (as outlined below), then we look to determine:

- Level 1: A satisfaction survey is distributed to find out if participants like the certification.
- Level 2: An assessment is used to determine if participants learned anything as a result of achieving the certification.
- Level 3: Behavior is observed to uncover if participants use the certification.
- Level 4: Results are reviewed to see if the certification has an effect.

If the Phillips model is applied with consideration to certification,

- Calculate ROI for certification similar to training programs. In fact, the model works well if we combine the two as one element.

Implementing a Tracking System for PDUs/CEUs

The following rationale holds for creating a system to track certification PDUs/CEUs:

- Allows the individual and organization to track certification-related training activities (i.e., courses taken, vendors used, hours trained) for the purpose of reporting
- Supports compliance requirements in the event any certifications are associated with regulatory audits
- Creates a history so the individual and organization have traceability for accounting purposes and metrics

There are several options that can be put into place to track PDUS/CEUs:

- Training records can be in the organization's learning management system (LMS).

- In some cases, only certain compliance courses are tracked on the LMS.
  - If the certificant wants the employer to maintain his or her training records, the training department can establish Microsoft Excel spreadsheets or a Microsoft Access database and put it in a shared-folder environment, such as Microsoft SharePoint.
  - Web-based database applications can provide enhanced capabilities for an electronic transcript.
- Some professional associations provide the service of storing PDUs/CEUs earned. Some offer certificants the capability of reporting on PDUs/CEUs earned and what is required for recertification or certification maintenance.

Note: The Compliance Advantage Learning Management System (CALMS) is included free of charge on the Resource CD for this book, in addition to other utilities that are designed to track PDUs/CEUs.

Assigning the Job Role to Oversee Professional Certification

Is it worth assigning the role and responsibility of professional development and certification to the department of training or HR? The answer is yes (see Table 7.1). *Note: In some organizations training is under HR or operations; it varies.*

Table 7.1   Considerations for Position in Training or Human Resources

Training Function	*Human Resources Function*
Chief learning officer	Chief human resources officer
Director of learning and performance	Human resources business partner
Associate director of training and development	Human resources practitioner
Manager of organizational learning	Talent management associate
Training and development specialist	Human capital representative
Learning management professional	Organizational development
Performance improvement trainer	Organizational effectiveness
Educational services officer	Human resources generalist
Learning and development partner	Human resources advocate

The key attributes for this position should utilize existing models, which include alignment with the competency models specified for professionals, such as:

- Training and development: American Society of Training and Development (ASTD)
- HR: Society of Human Resource Management (SHRM)

The professional development consultant has two roles:

- Coach: help employees to be more competitive and develop a winning attitude
- Mentor: show empathy and focus on what is in the person's best interest

The dynamics of what goes on in the military takes on a different process than for businesses or organizations. For example, in the Navy, the educational services officer (ESO) is responsible for the training and development function. The ESO is involved in instructional design, curriculum development, exam coordination, and more. The ESO advises personnel about the availability of voluntary education programs, such as certification, and may encourage them to enroll in these programs. The ESO assists personnel in applying for certification programs. For example, the ESO supports personnel requests to obtain vocational/technical certification, high school diplomas, and college degrees. The ESO is the liaison and key point of contact between the command and the Navy College Office supporting the command. The ESO will use various means to publicize certification opportunities, such as ship and station newspapers and the plan of the day. Certification courses will typically be viewed as nonresident training courses (NRTCs).

The eight-button analysis model, designed by the Hartt Peformance Group and an adaptation of Gilbert's behavior engineering model (BEM), can be instruments for groups such as the Navy and Coast Guard to implement certification. The human performance technology (HPT) concept here is that you determine which button needs to be pushed to receive the desired response from the individual:

- Organizational performance: information, resources, incentives, selection assignment
- Individual performance: knowledge, skills, motivation, capacity

The thought process here is that certification is all about improving performance.

Reviewing Implementability Concerns

Implementability refers to the practicality of introducing a new certification program or modifying an existing one (with major changes). Both the professional associations or professional organizations and certificant have a vested interest in implementability. *Note:* What is impractical for one professional associations or professional organizations may be practical for another professional associations or professional organizations. Implementability seeks to answer the question of which factors should be considered regarding this certification being made available:

- Should it be offered? Yes/No
- When should it be offered? Now, in the future, or never
- Why should it be offered? What is the reason for it? Will someone else do it?
- Where should it be offered? Should it be at a local, state, national, or global basis?
- How should it be offered? Will instruction be instructor led or self-study?
- To whom should it be offered? Which groups should be included?

Implementability should not be a rush decision, quickly concluding that a professional associations or professional organizations should avoid offering a certification because it will be, for example:

- Time consuming (require a long period to complete)
- Require many resources (i.e., people, systems, facilities)
- Large in scope (i.e., offered on an international basis)

Implementability is concerned with the risks that are associated with offering a new certification program. It looks at the possible outcomes associated with uncertainties. It is an if/then analysis or risk assessment. Implementability is situation specific based on risk versus reward. If a professional associations or professional organizations is risk averse, then it will be reluctant to offer the certification.

If a professional associations or professional organizations determines that a certification program has potential and its investment is justified, it may address risk through:

- Acceptance (moving forward): understanding the issues and being okay with them
- Mitigation (lessening the impact): minimizing the up-front investment by creating only the deliverables initially required
- Transference (insurance policy): third-party vendors assume most of the liability, which may be represented by giving the vendor more opportunity to generate revenue
- Avoidance (delay): waiting to offer the certification until there is an increased demand

Factors that are related to implementability include:

- Accountability: who will be responsible and for what

- Desirability: how much the professional associations or professional organizations, occupation, and people want it
- Disposability: what is involved if the certification needs to be discontinued
- Maintainability: what will be required to monitor the success of the program
- Manageability: how effective the professional associations or professional organizations can be in administration tasks
- Marketability: how profitable the certification will be
- Portability: which new locations or groups could utilize this certification
- Predictability: how accurate the forecast can be regarding potential certificants
- Sustainability: what is necessary to grow the program to ensure it is healthy
- Transferability: what content can be taken from this certification and used in another
- Usability: what instrumental use will the certification have on the job
- Vulnerability: what other professional associations or professional organizations will be a competitor now or in the future

Sustaining Accreditation with a Recognized Authority

At the end of the day, whether it is a certification program or an association management company, the goal is a seal of approval from the occupation or industry. Associations may seek accreditation through agencies such as the National Commission for Certifying Agencies (NCCA), whereas association management companies seek accreditation through the Association Management Companies Institute (AMCI). How does this work?

Q: What types of certification are accredited?
A: The NCCA, for example, accredits the certification programs and not the association. The NCCA standards are only for personnel (individuals) certification.
Q: How long does it take for a certification program to become accredited?
A: The time it takes for a certification program to become accredited through NCCA will vary.
Q: What does the process involve to become accredited?
A: The process entails submitting an application online to the NCCA. There are three annual deadlines. Commissioners review the applications and discuss their findings in person approximately 2 to 3 months following the deadline. A response is received in 3 to 4 months after the review and is expedited because the online review also allows a quick notification. Applications may be approved, deferred, or denied.
Q: How much testing is required for accreditation?
A: There is a requirement of 500 candidates tested or implementation of 1 year before an application for accreditation may be accepted. This is due to

program maturity and need for statistical analyses to provide information on reliability and validity of the assessment instruments. A program that has been developed carefully will have conducted market research and the like before seeking accreditation.

Q: What are the costs associated with accreditation of a certification program?

A: As of January 2013, application fees were $1,600 for a member of the Institute for Credentialing Excellence (ICE) and $2,125 for nonmembers. Multiple applications submitted for the same deadline will incur fees of $800 each. Then, there are annual dues to maintain accreditation, which include ICE membership. One to two programs are $3,875/year, with $800 for each additional program up to a maximum of $10,275/year.

Q: What if the certification does not meet NCCA standards?

A: If substantive deficiencies are noted as they relate to compliance with the NCCA standards, these deficiencies are not generally easily or quickly correctable.

Q: Where is guidance on certification provided?

A: With the NCCA's online system, there is considerable guidance provided regarding what is necessary to demonstrate compliance to each standard so that those seeking accreditation have sufficient understanding of the rigor involved in achieving and maintaining accreditation before they submit an application.

Q: How much is the tool to conduct the evaluation?

A: The tool is available at no charge. A free self-assessment checklist is available on the website to help programs gauge their readiness.

Q: Why are applications deferred?

A: Most often, an application may be deferred because there was insufficient evidence provided to demonstrate full compliance to one or more standards, but the necessary compliance can be achieved within 90 days.

Q: Where can someone to find out if a certification program has been accredited?

A: The list of accredited programs is available online (http://www.credentialing excellence.org).

Many association management companies have strived to maintain quality as they support professional associations. For a long period of time, AMCs worked with ASAE and AMCI. From 2001 to 2010, ASAE awarded AMC accreditation to AMCs that maintained accreditation requirements. This accreditation program from ASAE ended on May 7, 2010, and the remaining accreditations were terminated on December 31, 2010. The purpose of this program was to heighten professional standards, promote quality, and identify AMCs that demonstrated the required knowledge of association management. ASAE no longer offers an accreditation program but does recognize AMCI's accreditation of AMCs.

AMCI has maintained an accreditation program for AMCs that adheres to the approved standard for good practices of the American National Standards

Institute (ANSI). What is expected of an AMC that has been accredited to the ANSI/AMCI Standard?

- Compliant accounting procedures with the Federal Accounting Standards Board (FASB)
- Documented record-keeping procedures
- Employee training programs that educate employees on the AMC's policies and procedures
- Adequate contract review and transition procedures
- Sufficient insurance coverage

Accreditation for an AMC can be a significant sales tool for working with a professional association. It also requires time and effort to maintain this accreditation. This does not necessarily imply that an AMC that is not accredited by AMCI does not meet these standards. What accreditation signifies is that if an AMC desires accreditation from AMCI, then it must comply with these standards. *Note:* Other agencies that offer accreditation that is of any value should have established rigorous standards.

Q: What if a professional associations or professional organizations does not seek accreditation but follows the recommended standards of an accrediting body?

A: This is a common issue, with many quality certification programs following the recommendations but not completing the accreditation process because it can be rigorous. Following the recommended standards of the accrediting body is a good thing. The question is how the professional associations or professional organizations draws attention to its adherence to these standards. In other words, does the professional associations or professional organizations make mention that it is following the standards, or does it just follow the standards? The key is that the professional associations or professional organizations does not misrepresent the standard (i.e., make it appear that it is accredited when it is in fact not).

Q: What avenues exist to help professional associations improve their quality of service?

A: If member dues and funding support from the headquarters are insufficient, the professional association may be challenged into fund-raising or obtaining grants. To this end, the Certified Fund Raising Executive (CFRE) certification focuses on higher-level competencies to address this skill. Alternatively, the Grant Professionals Certification Institute™ (GPCI) administers the Grant Professional Certification (GPC). The GPC measures the certificant's ability to provide quality grant-related services within an ethical framework. It was established in 2004 by the Grant Professionals Association (GPA).

Q: Is certification needed for fund-raising or grant writing?

A: While certification is not needed for fund-raising or grant writing in every instance, these activities can definitely benefit from someone with expertise in these areas.

Adhering to Sound Instructional Design and Curriculum Development

Sound instructional design and curriculum development refers to processes that are used to ensure certification training materials adequately support the learning objectives so that people are prepared to pass the certification exam. People use a variety of paths to pursue certification, so there must be clarity regarding who is in control of the training. Many times, it becomes a combination of the service provider and customization of materials. The sources include:

- professional associations or professional organizations
- Vendors who have been contracted to develop certification study material
- Facilitators or designated trainers using the materials

How is training on a certification program delivered?

- In person and facilitated by an instructor
- Self-study through reading material
- Virtually through group participation or accessing online content

Many organizations make the necessary investment and identify an authorized vendor who can provide high-quality certification training. For example, for Microsoft certification, Advison has been recognized as a premier solutions provider and can deliver off-the-shelf solutions or customize the courseware to support specialized requirements. Some individuals may be under budget constraints and will create their own materials and study groups to save on course costs, or companies may host their own internal education sessions to support certification education. Companies such as True Solutions create high-quality media that enable these individuals to build their own training materials and facilitate study group sessions using training aids.

There are a number of industry standard approaches that can be followed to ensure that instruction design and curriculum development (IDCD) adheres to good practices:

- ADDIE (analysis, design, develop, implement, evaluate): the traditional approach to instructional design
  - Analysis: explore training and development objectives and determine gaps

- Design: define learning objectives, content, delivery method, and assessments
- Develop: create content (i.e., storyboards, slides, graphics, video, audio, etc.)
- Implement: pilot and roll out the training.
- Evaluate: measure effectiveness or efficiency of training deliverables
■ SAM: successive approximation model (ADDIE alternative)
    - Preparation phase (information gathering): background
    - Iterative design phase (savvy start, project planning, additional design): design, prototype, review
    - Iterative development phase (design proof, alpha, beta, gold): develop, implement, evaluate
■ ADDSUP (assess, define, develop, show, umpire, publish): the IDCD model created by Willis Thomas recommended for certificate and certification programs:
    - Assess: understand the requirements through needs analysis
    - Define: agree and document the approach and next steps
    - Develop: create and refine the prototype
    - Show: let people see what it will initially look like
    - Umpire: invite critical review from subject matter experts
    - Publish: launch training in the appropriate stage (i.e., alpha, beta, or final)

Since the early 2000s, the e-learning industry has experienced tremendous growth. This is in part due to introduction of rapid development tools, such as Adobe Presenter, Lectora, and Articulate, which enable nonprogrammers to create dynamic e-learning content quickly and affordably.

These e-learning tools incorporate the desired basic functionality for most training applications; however, there is sometimes a compromise in the advanced features needed to ensure training compliance. Compliance requirements are particularly important when certification is involved.

According to Kingsley (2013), an experienced e-learning solutions expert, most e-learning programs now have the capability to create an assessment, but many are limited when it comes to accurately determining a learner's true knowledge of the subject matter. His company (https://elearningenhanced.com) in 2012 created a unique solution for a medical training company that had a requirement to certify a learner's ability to quickly and accurately assess patients. The scenario involved a patient coming on screen, with the learner clicking areas to learn about the patient and then selecting the best care option.

A second desired requirement was to test response speed; this functionality was not inherent in the standard features of the e-learning program. What was needed was a robust timing function. The company's research indicated that some tools will let you set a timer for the question, but it will be marked incorrect if the timer runs out. In this case, the learner could be correct no matter how long it took to answer the question, but the score needed to be scaled based on how long it actually took the user to respond. A custom solution was developed that could be added to the built-in scenario. HTML5 was integrated to create a timer that runs as the learner considers the options. Points can now be awarded for timeliness and correctness. This solution makes the e-learning more engaging.

Another requirement that elearningenhanced.com has encountered involves integrity with assessments (i.e., multiple-choice quizzes). Their customers have inquired about the ability of the e-learning program to prevent cheating. One common trick some dishonest people have used when attempting to cheat involved gaining access to the e-learning and skipping through it to print certificates in their own name without successfully completing the training and passing the assessment. There are a number of ways this has been accomplished. Unfortunately, many e-learning programs do not adhere to strict course progression rules (i.e., complete module A before module B) or certificate printing restrictions. As a result, some users are able to circumvent the system and print certificates, which make it appear they were fully trained. In response to this training dilemma, some experienced course developers have created completion verification by adding rules (i.e., tracking each slide viewed or controlling certificate printing).

But, because these advanced tools are not built into many standard products or are not designed to work in any hosting environment, they are not capable of performing basic security checks. For example, a common practice is for the course to request the learner to input his or her name prior to printing the certificate of completion. This enables one learner to revisit that section of the course many times and input other people's names. For this problem, elearningenhanced.com created a custom script that communicates with the hosting environment and pulls the user's name from the secure server rather than simply asking for it. Usually, the learner is logged in to an LMS, website, corporate network, or the like, so this is a viable solution. After examining that environment and log-in options, the e-learning is configured so that it can access the code that will inquire of the LMS, site, or network for the current user's name and then put *only* that name on the certificate.

As developers push the envelope on e-learning, they create interactive games, virtual environments, and simulations. Users can dial into servers or cloud-based services and access training on certification programs. There are a series of programs that support this development effort, such as HTML5, Adobe Flash, Smith Micro Poser, and Articulate Storyline.

Flashvalley.com is a premier developer of this type of e-learning content. It is a popular website and Flash community dedicated to Adobe Flash and Actionscript development. Flashvalley components have been featured on the CD-ROM of the magazine *Web Designer* (Imagine publishing) (issues 165, 167, and 168) in the United States, United Kingdom, France, and Germany. Calwen (2013), the founder of Flashvalley.com, emphasizes that computers, tablets, and smartphones are *simply* tools; we should not adapt to them, but rather, as a natural extension of our needs, they should adapt to us and not intimidate. The creative developer's mission is to initiate or reconcile the user with the interactive experience; a good developer is the bridge between the machine and the user. This developer will either succeed in engaging the user or widen the chasm.

Calwen (2013) states he likes to involve clients in the development process as it can bring new ideas to the table, and they often realize that "there was a lot more to it" than initially anticipated. The popularization of tablets and smartphones has opened the door to a world of development possibilities, and it is an exciting time for creative developers. This should result in developing certification programs that are engaging and can be accessed at any time using virtually any communications device. Calwen feels that simplicity will be key in the development of interactive content. He states that we live in a world where "more" is considered best and predicts a future in which minimalism and simplicity will prevail.

Suggested Reading

Dalton, J., and Dignam, M. (2007). *The Decision to Join: How Individuals Determine Value and Why They Choose to Belong*. Washington, DC: ASAE and the Center for Association Leadership.

Educational Services Officer Fundamentals. (n.d.). Retrieved February 2013 from http://navyadministration.tpub.com/14083a/css/14083a_11.htm.

Grettenberger, J. (2013). *Five Tips to Get IT Auditors Off Your Back*. White paper. Aliso Viejo, CA: Dell Software.

Knapp, J., Anderson, L., and Wild, C. (2009). *Certification: The ICE Handbook*, 2nd ed. Washington, DC: Institute for Credentialing Excellence.

Chapter 8

Case Studies in Professional Certification

Key Lessons

- Spotlight examples of professional certifications:
  - Association for Operation Management (APICS)
  - American Society for Quality (ASQ)
  - American Society for Training and Development (ASTD)
  - American Society of Association Executives (ASAE)
  - Association of Clinical Research Professionals (ACRP)
  - Cisco Learning Network
  - International Institute for Learning (IIL)
  - International Society for Performance Improvement (ISPI)
  - Microsoft
  - Project Management Institute (PMI)
  - Society for Human Resources Management (SHRM)

Technical journals have a major influence on the ratings of professional certification. In 2012, Techrepublic.com published the following list of the 10 best information technology (IT) certifications:

1. MCITP: Microsoft Certified IT Professional
2. MCTS: Microsoft Certified Technology Specialist
3. VCP: VMware Certified Professional
4. CCNA: Cisco Certified Network Associate

5. CSSA: Certified SonicWall Security Administrator
6. PMP: Project Management Professional
7. CISSP: Certified Information Systems Security Professional
8. ACSP: Apple Certified Support Professional
9. Network+/A+
10. CompTIA Healthcare IT Technician

Association for Operations Management

APICS is the global leader and premier source of the body of knowledge in supply chain and operations management, including production, inventory, materials management, purchasing, and logistics. The APICS education and certification programs are recognized worldwide as the standard of professional competence in production and inventory management and supply chain and operations management.

It was founded in 1957 as the American Production and Inventory Control Society. Since 1957, individuals and companies have relied on APICS for its superior training, internationally recognized certifications, comprehensive resources and worldwide network of accomplished industry professionals. More than 98,000 individuals have earned the APICS Certified in Production and Inventory Management (CPIM) designation, and more than 13,000 individuals have earned their APICS Certified Supply Chain Professional (CSCP) designation.

The APICS Certified in Production and Inventory Management (CPIM) program provides individuals with the ability to understand and evaluate production and inventory activities within a company's global operations. Since 1973, more than 98,000 professionals worldwide have earned their APICS CPIM designation, making it the preferred certification for thousands of employers. Advancing Productivity, Innovation, and Competitive Success (APICS) has been the new tag line adopted by this organization.

The APICS CPIM designation is earned upon successful completion of exams covering the following five modules.

Basics of Supply Chain Management

The basic concepts in managing the complete flow of materials in a supply chain from suppliers to customers are covered in the Basics module. This module covers manufacturing, distribution, service, and retail industries. This includes the fundamental relationships in the design, planning, execution, monitoring, and control that occur. Knowledge of the material in this module is assumed as a prerequisite for the other APICS CPIM modules, which cover similar topics in much greater depth. Topics include:

- Understanding basic business-wide concepts, including understanding various supply chain environments
- Managing demand, including markets and customer expectations
- Designing products, processes, and information systems
- Understanding supply issues including inventory costs, functions, and metrics

Master Planning of Resources

Explore and be able to apply the principles of demand management, sales and operations planning, master scheduling, and distribution planning, and to identify conditions that require action. This module evaluates knowledge of both supply and demand planning for mid- to long-term independent demand. Topics include:

- Recognizing all demands for goods and services to support the marketplace
- Bringing together all the plans for the business
- Disaggregating the production plan into an executable schedule
- Planning the distribution network and replenishment

Detailed Scheduling and Planning

Acquire a working knowledge of the tools and techniques for planning of inventory, including planning techniques such as MRP, CRP, lean, TOC, and projects. Understand the effect of using each technique; know standard measurements for inventory, materials, capacity and supplier performance; and recognize when to escalate issues. Topics include:

- Managing inventory, planning material requirements, planning capacity requirements, and procurement and supplier planning
- Recognizing the importance of supply chain management and deploying supply chain strategies related to scheduling, planning, and sourcing
- Translating product-level plans and schedules generated at the master planning level into requirements that can be procured or produced
- Bridging the master planning area with the execution and control function
- Planning, scheduling, resource allocation, and implementing projects that are used to manage the supply of products and services

Execution and Control of Operations

Learn to translate plans into operational activities and define and apply techniques in the operations field. Topics include:

■ Comparing actual output to plans and taking appropriate corrective actions
■ Communicating ideas in a group setting and instructing others in tasks
■ Creating operational solutions in the face of competing resources
■ Explaining the release of work and reporting performance through data collection
■ Understanding the execution of quality initiatives and continuous improvement plans
■ Evaluating trade-offs and participating in design decisions

Strategic Management of Resources

Move your learning to the next level through the SMR module that includes higher-level thinking or strategic planning and implementation of operations. This includes an understanding of how market requirements drive the resources and processes of an organization. Topics include:

■ Understanding concepts that require a combination of elements and higher thinking within the entire CPIM body of knowledge
■ Knowing the relationship of existing and emerging processes and technologies to operations and supply chain functions
■ Understanding various business environments
■ Knowing how business strategies are developed and how operation strategies are implemented

The APICS CSCP program helps individuals demonstrate their knowledge and organizational skills for developing more streamlined operations. Since its launch in 2006, more than 13,000 professionals in 77 countries have earned the APICS CSCP designation.

The APICS CSCP designation is the most widely recognized educational program for supply chain and operations management professionals around the globe. It is a designation that is sought by thousands of employers and recruiters and provides designees with a mastery of supply chain management best practices that distinguishes them as industry experts with specialized, high-level knowledge and skills.

The APICS CSCP exam consists of three important modules. The exam reflects critical changes in the marketplace and in the evolving roles and responsibilities of operations and supply chain managers. For accreditation, individuals must master each of the following:

■ **MODULE 1:** APICS Supply Chain Management Fundamentals
  – Broad concepts include primary processes, objectives, logistics, integration methods, and rewards

- Alignment of supply chain with corporate strategies
- Key considerations for planning, inventory control, and continued improvement
- Identification and management of market segments
- Demand forecasting and effective management techniques
- Effective customer relationship management (CRM)
■ **MODULE 2:** Supply Chain Strategy, Design, and Compliance
- Sustainability practices in design and operation
- Measurement, responsiveness, operations, and communications
- Risk, its sources, impacts, and mitigation methods
- Globally dispersed supply and demand, and the effects on logistics
- Factors influencing demand, including design, marketing, selling, and matching customer orders
- Core Customer Relationship Management (CRM) concepts, including strategies, technologies, and implementation challenges
- Fundamentals of supplier relationship management (SRM), including strategies, improved source management, relevant technologies, and measurement
- Inventory planning and control methods
■ **MODULE 3:** Implementation and Operations
- Supply chain dynamics and the balance of responsiveness and efficiency
- Managing supply from internal and external sources
- Implementation of demand plans, including prioritization, fulfillment, and capturing and communicating point-of-sale data
- Tools and techniques to support continuous improvement

American Society for Quality

The American Society for Quality (ASQ) is a global community of people dedicated to quality who share the ideas and tools that make our world work better. With millions of individual and organizational members of the community in 150 countries, ASQ has the reputation and reach to bring together the diverse quality champions who are transforming the world's corporations, organizations, and communities to meet tomorrow's critical challenges. ASQ is headquartered in Milwaukee, Wisconsin, with national service centers in China, India, and Mexico. Established in 1946, ASQ started offering certifications in 1968. The Certified Quality Engineer (CQE) was the first program that ASQ offered. Since then, more than 170,000 individuals around the world have become ASQ certified. More than 125 global companies have formally recognized ASQ's certifications as verification of an individual's knowledge of quality theory and techniques. ASQ certification is peer recognition that an individual has demonstrated proficiency in, and comprehension of, a particular quality area at a specific point in time. To receive ASQ certification candidates must:

1. Have a specified level of education or experience;
2. Provide proof of professionalism;
3. Pass a standardized exam in the certification area.

Today, ASQ offers 17 certifications, all of which are viewed as an essential development tool to help quality professionals stand out in the workplace. Programs range from the basics of quality and Statistical Process Control (SPC) for the (Certified Quality Improvement Associate and the Certified Quality Process Analyst) to a Quality Inspector and Technician, CQE, Reliability Engineer, Quality Auditor, through the Certified Manager of Quality and Organizational Excellence. ASQ also provides a wide range of Six Sigma certifications, from the Green Belt and Black Belt to the Master Black Belt.

American Society for Training and Development

Founded in 1943, the American Society for Training and Development (ASTD) is the world's largest association dedicated to training and development professionals. ASTD has created an outstanding staff that consistently demonstrates customer focus and professionalism. ASTD's website and conferences are regarded as world class and provide unique venues for professional development. ASTD's members come from more than 100 countries and connect locally in more than 120 U.S. chapters and with more than 15 international partners. Members work in thousands of organizations of all sizes, in government, as independent consultants, and as suppliers. In recent years ASTD has widened the profession's focus to link learning and performance to individual and organizational results and is a sought-after voice on critical public policy issues.

To support members' ongoing development in the field, ASTD formed the ASTD Certification Institute (ASTD CI) to take the lead in setting professional industry standards and to certify training and development professionals through credentialing. ASTD CI built the Certified Professional in Learning and Performance® (CPLP®) credential to provide a way for training and development professionals to prove their value to employers and to be confident about their knowledge of the field. ASTD's CPLP certification program aligns the test content to the areas of expertise identified by the ASTD Competency Model. Key value propositions with respect to the CPLP credential, as it pertains to the individual, helps:

1. Industry advancement and opportunity
2. Credibility

3. Commitment to the profession, and
4. Demonstrated competence and performance

ASTD CI administers the program and has awarded the CPLP designation to training and development professionals since 2006. ASTD's CPLP exam was designed within NCCA (National Commission for Certifying Agencies) guidelines and has been psychometrically proven to be valid and reliable. The CPLP program has achieved a number of milestones that have led up to its current level of success:

- 2004: ASTD launches the ASTD Competency Study (Mapping the Future)
- 2005: ASTD CI launches CPLP pilot program based on the 2004 model
- 2006: ASTD releases the ASTD Learning System (self-study materials) and ASTD CI launches the CPLP operational program
- 2007: ASTD CI completes first CPLP operational year (July 2007)
- 2009: ASTD CI recertifies first wave of CPLP credential holders
- 2010: Global expansion strategy completed; first global expansion partner selected
- 2011: Global expansion pilot program launched with partner
- 2012: Global expansion operational program launched with partner; ASTD Competency Model (Talent Redefined™) completed
- 2013: Launched revised ASTD Competency Model

There are now more than 1,635 companies posting CPLP preferred job opportunities, based on combined counts from ASTD Job Bank and Monster.com. Moreover, there are many other job engines, such as CareerBuilder and employer websites, that have identified the CPLP certification as highly sought after in their job advertisements. There are many companies that have recognized the CPLP as a best practice. This is due to the increasing importance of learning and development professionals achieving professional certification.

There were a total of nearly 1,200 current and active CPLPs as of YE12 (2006–2012). The CPLP means confidence, credibility, and market advantage. The CPLP is the differentiator many employers look for when they seek someone who possesses expertise and demonstrates what it takes to link training to organizational performance. The Certified Professional in Learning and Performance credential can only be earned by those with at least three years of experience in the field, who must pass a rigorous knowledge test and in-depth work product. CPLP credential holders have instant credibility and an advantage in the job market. Organizations with CPLPs on staff have an assurance that their training professionals have the necessary knowledge and expertise across the entire breadth of the field. Some of the additional benefits of CPLP certification are:

- Improved training compliance
- Standardized training project management

- Enhanced instructional design and curriculum development processes
- Increased morale on training teams
- Focused professional development for training staff
- Expanded network to training professionals on a global basis

The CPLP program was shaped in accordance with testing industry standards to ensure the integrity and quality of the program. The question of whether ASTD CI should pursue ANSI (American National Standards Institute) or NCCA accreditation for the CPLP program was raised in 2012. The general consensus was that continuing to align to the standards was beneficial for the integrity and quality of the program, even if ASTD CI should choose not to pursue accreditation in the near future. This decision was made in alignment with ASTD CI's program strategies.

American Society of Association Executives

The American Trade Association Executives (ATAE) was founded and later became the American Society of Association Executives (ASAE). It began with 67 charter members. ASAE now has more than 25,000 individual members who manage leading trade, professional, and philanthropic associations. ASAE now represents more than 10,000 associations serving more than 287 million people and organizations globally. ASAE helps associations grow through educational programs and collaboration. Their research arm engages in very interesting studies that uncover what associations must do to remain successful.

ASAE's Certified Association Executive (CAE) was introduced by ASAE in 1960. It began as an essay exam and matured into a psychometrically valid multiple-choice exam. In 2003, the CAE exam was revised to align the concepts with actual issues encountered by association executives. The CAE certification has become highly desirable for many association executives to achieve. It is now a 200-item multiple-choice test composed of nine domain areas:

- Organizational management
- Leadership
- Administration
- Knowledge management and research
- Governance and structure
- Public policy, government relations, and coalition building
- Membership development
- Programs, products, and services
- Marketing, public relations, and communications

The CAE program was accredited by NCCA in 2010. In order to sit for the CAE exam, the individual must satisfy educational and experience requirements:

- Experience requirements for association management as specified on ASAE's website at www.asaecenter.org
- A university degree or 5 years experience (if no college degree)
- Complete the five Certified Association Executive (CAE) courses
- Successfully pass the Certified Association Executive (CAE) exam

ASAE also supports professional development of association members through ASAE University. It addresses functional areas of association management, leadership, and governance.

ASAE University offers in-person instructor-led courses, certificate programs, and online programs for staff at various levels and association leaders.

Association of Clinical Research Professionals

The Association of Clinical Research Professionals (ACRP) was founded in 1976 and has become the primary resource for clinical research professionals in the pharmaceutical, biotechnology, and medical device industries and those in hospital, academic medical centers, and physician office settings. Their website, acrpnet. org, details the benefits and requirements of being certified in three key roles of clinical research: clinical research coordinator (CCRC˚), clinical research associate (CCRA˚), and physician investigator (CPI˚).

The certification process, which requires applicants to demonstrate extensive hands-on work performing duties essential to the specific job function in which they wish to be certified, validates a candidate's clinical research knowledge, skills, and the application of those skills through a comprehensive written examination and mandates ongoing professional development in clinical research topics in order to retain one's certification.

Over 26,500 individuals in 53 nations have become certified through ACRP since the inception of the CCRC program in 1992. Over 20 years later, the CCRC, CCRA, and CPI programs are the only National Commission for Certifying Agencies (NCCA)-accredited programs operating in the clinical research space. NCCA accreditation attests to the validity and credibility of the certification programs. ACRP uses a comprehensive job-analysis process, updated approximately every 5 years, to validate the knowledge, skills, and abilities required of various clinical research professionals and to ensure that its certification exams are testing current practice.

In addition, test questions are written by currently practicing, certified clinical research professionals and the exams are put together by a group of role-specific subject matter experts who are also currently certified to ensure the standards of the program keep pace with shifts and changes in the industry.

Recognized by a wide number of employer groups for recruitment, retention, and recognition purposes, the ACRP certification programs focus on the globally accepted International Conference on Harmonization (ICH) guidelines, recognizing those guidelines as the foundation for most country-specific regulation around clinical research. This sets the ACRP programs apart as globally portable credentials and a medium for establishing a globally recognized standard of competency. Additional benefits include improving career opportunities and advancement; increasing job satisfaction; and demonstrating engagement in one's chosen career path. Additionally, ACRP certification must be maintained every 2 years, requiring ongoing clinical research-specific professional development and involvement.

This association has done an outstanding job in filling an important role for certification. They have a quality website, journal, forums, certification programs, and knowledgeable staff to support it.

Cisco Learning Network

Learning@Cisco, a business unit of Cisco, is dedicated to supporting the growth of networks and helping individuals gain the information technology skills to design, build, install, and maintain those networks worldwide. Cisco believes that services from trained, qualified individuals make the difference in who has the technological edge today, and the company uses education as a strategic asset to help grow its business and the overall industry. Over the past 20 years, Learning@Cisco has developed technology training to help transform learners from holding minimal IT knowledge to in-depth IT skills. Cisco's industry-leading certification program outlines every technology role in the networking industry and maps out roles by levels and specializations.

Cisco's first certification program, the highly respected Cisco Certified Internetwork Export (CCIE®) expert-level certification, was conceived in the Cisco Technical Assistance Center (TAC) when engineers handling support calls recognized a need to train more experts. Certifications first conceived for experts quickly grew to include offerings for entry-level and professional-level networking practitioners.

From the original CCIE certification, today's offerings include more than 40 programs and 2 million certified experts and associates and professionals encompassing employees, partners, and customers. Cisco offers online training for everything in its product portfolio. Cisco has continued to offer new training and certification programs in data center, video, and service provider and a complete refresh of security, wireless, routing, and switching. Cisco's website is very comprehensive and addresses benefits of hiring a Cisco Certified Professional, Cisco IT Certification and Career Paths, the Cisco Learning Partner program, and ways to stay connected such as the Cisco LinkedIn Certifications Group.

Through its Networking Academy® and Learning Partner programs, Cisco embeds programs into schools and educational companies, providing learning material through the online Cisco Learning Network, and connecting students with instructors. Key components of Cisco's learning ecosystem, which reaches 1.2 million students annually, include:

■ The Networking Academy was established in 1997 and now counts more than one million students worldwide and 10,000 academies in 165 countries. The Networking Academy public-private partnership model creates the "world's largest classroom." Cisco partners with educational institutions, nonprofits and nongovernmental organizations, governments, and community centers to provide classroom space, computer lab equipment, and qualified instructors. Cisco also provides online curricula, teacher training, and professional development for instructors free of charge.

■ More than 500 Cisco Learning Partners deliver Cisco authorized training to over 400,000 customers and channel partners on an annual basis via all types of modalities, along the lines of both technical training and enablement and business readiness. The Cisco Learning Network website has more than 70 million page views in one year and more than a half million registered users. The site offers career advice and student networking, connections to news events, game arcades and resources, an outline of certifications and self-assessments, resources including a technology library and learning lounges, and a store.

■ Cisco Press sells 300,000 books per year as well as videos and other electronic learning tools. Pearson VUE helps Cisco develop technical books that are translated and distributed worldwide.

International Institute for Learning

With wholly owned operating companies in 18 countries and clients in more than 150 countries, the International Institute for Learning (IIL) is a global leader in training, consulting, coaching, and customized course development. IIL's core competencies include project, program, and portfolio management; Microsoft® Project and Project Server; business analysis; Lean Six Sigma; Information Technology Infrastructure Library (ITIL®); leadership and interpersonal skills; and corporate consciousness and sustainability. IIL delivers innovative, effective, and consistent training solutions through a variety of learning approaches, including virtual classroom, traditional classroom, simulation training, interactive on-demand training, video, and a blended approach. IIL has more than 350 international trainers in 35 countries, who deliver courses in more than 25 languages.

IIL is in its 22nd year of doing business. It is the learning solution provider of choice for many top global companies, including 6 of the 10 largest banks in the world, 3 of the 5 largest software companies in the world, and 6 of the 10 largest companies in the United States. IIL is a PMI® (Project Management Institute) Charter Global Registered Education Provider, a member of PMI's

Global Executive Council, a Microsoft Partner (with a Microsoft Gold Project and Portfolio Management competency), an IIBA˚ Endorsed Education Provider, and an APMG Accredited Training Organization (ATO) for PRINCE2˚ and ITIL. IIL also provides training for APMG certifications, including Agile project management, management of portfolios, managing successful programs, management of risk, and portfolio, program, and project offices.

IIL is certified as a Women's Business Enterprise (WBE) by the Women's Business Enterprise Council (WBENC) and was recognized in six categories as a 2011 Top Business by DiversityBusiness.com.

IIL offers joint certificate programs with its two prestigious university affiliates: New York University's School of Continuing and Professional Studies (NYU-SCPS) and University of Southern California's Marshall School of Business (USC-MSB). The three key values that define the IIL brand are intelligence, integrity, and innovation. IIL focuses on creating customer loyalty and building enduring relationships. Strengths that have earned IIL a reputation as a front-runner in the learning industry include:

- A belief that learning must yield practical, quantifiable benefits to have value, which is why all of its courses integrate training approaches that are easy to understand and assimilate. Curriculum must be designed to engage critical thinking skills and give real-world knowledge that can be taken back and applied in the work environment.
- Program evaluations point overwhelmingly to the excellence of IIL's trainers. IIL holds its staff to the highest standards of professionalism, and its expert facilitation skills complement extensive industry and classroom experience.
- To cater to diverse learning styles and preferences, IIL uses Many Methods of Learning™ to deliver courses and programs. Clients choose the approach that best aligns with their needs and their schedule.
- Global presence gives customers the opportunity to leverage the power of IIL's wholly owned network of companies, strategically located worldwide. IIL has deep experience working in different languages, cultures, countries, and industries and is proud it has been selected as a learning solution partner by many top global companies.

IIL prides itself on being a client-driven company. It delivers on that every day, investing the time and energy needed to grow the profession as well as its business. It works closely with clients—asking, listening, and responding with new courses and tools. IIL provides a dedicated support team 24 x 5 Monday–Friday (ET) to address any client technical challenges. This ensures that participants in virtual courses experience real-time quality customer support.

IIL believes in a holistic approach to learning as a process and offers its clients all the key building blocks necessary to achieve excellence in vital project processes, including:

- Assessment tools such as the Kerzner Project Management Maturity Model (KPM3)
- 360° Project Management Competency Assessment (360° PMCA™)
- Needs analysis to define gaps and to address the organizational and process changes needed to fill them
- Measurement of efficiency and productivity performance, including changes in team behavior, return on investment for training and development initiatives, and specific key performance metrics in project management, Lean Six Sigma, and business analysis
- Group coaching and individual mentoring to ensure that classroom lessons are actually put into practice and integrated into the daily work practice
- Process development and improvement through direct, hands-on support or knowledge management solutions such as IIL's Unified Project Management® Methodology (UPMM™), which ensures enterprise-wide consistency and quality in project, program, and portfolio management implementation

International Society for Performance Improvement

As a pioneer in the field, the International Society for Performance Improvement (ISPI) understood the strength and value of performance-based certification long before any organization would consider the model. According to the *Standards for Educational and Psychological Testing* published by the American Educational Research Association, "Tests are widely used in the credentialing of persons for many occupations and professions. . . . Certification plays a similar role in many occupations not regulated by governments and is often a necessary precursor to advancement in many occupations. Certification has also become widely used to indicate that a person has certain specific skills … or knowledge … which may only be a part of their occupational duties" (p. 156). When the word *test* is used, many immediately think of knowledge exams and classroom instruction. However, ISPI's performance-based certification, Certified Performance Technologist (CPT), is a test, but of real-world experience and results.

"While a primary goal of employment testing is the accurate prediction of subsequent job behaviors or job outcomes, it is important to recognize that there are limits to degree to which such criteria can be predicted" (American Educational Research Association, p. 155). By recognizing the limitations of knowledge tests, ISPI's performance-based certification process allows candidates to show how they successfully demonstrated worthy performance by applying a sustainable, systematic approach to their work. Earning the CPT designation is not about taking classes or passing a test. It is about delivering service that clients value and doing it in a way that can be measured and replicated.

"The CPT designation represents recognition by the leading performance improvement professional society for real-world application of the performance technology and achievement of valuable results for clients" (Carol M. Panza, CPT). Regarding the history of CPT, on November 13–14, 2000, ISPI convened a presidential task force to begin the development of the process and standards for a performance-based certification. The task force included more than 30 individuals from industry, government, and academia, as well as independent practitioners. They were tasked with developing a certification that would assist employers and clients in distinguishing practitioners who had proven they could produce results through a systematic process and allow practitioners to assess their capability, better focus their professional development efforts, and recognize their capability. As a result, the 10 standards of performance technology were developed and validated by Indiana University graduate students through an extensive literature review to confirm the standards appeared in practice, and the CPT was launched in 2002.

> The CPT standards have served as valuable guiding posts for my professional work. When I brainstorm, have doubts about my strategies, or need to make decisions, I go back to the standards, and they always help me to make the right decisions. What I do must add value, and great solutions cannot be born in a vacuum but a through partnership with customer. (Hozumi Kessler, CPT)

The CPT designation recognizes practitioners who have demonstrated proficiency in 10 standards of performance technology in ways that are in keeping with ISPI's code of ethics. Candidates for the CPT are required to have 3 years of experience and describe at least three examples of how their work exemplifies the use of the 10 standards. The projects in the application are blind and peer reviewed by CPTs trained in the review process.

ISPI has reviewers qualified in at least 12 of the most common languages, like Italian, Portuguese, Spanish, Chinese, and so forth. This provides the necessary flexibility as ISPI's certification reaches beyond the borders of North America, with CPTs in 31 countries. In addition, there are reviewers who have the highest security clearances required by the U.S. government.

In late 2012, ISPI received confirmation of the value of its performance-based certification when the U.S. Agency for International Development launched an RFP, "Human and Institutional Capacity Development for Non-Critical Priority Countries," which noted preference of CPTs to fulfill certain project roles (U.S. Agency for International Development [USAID] Bureau for Economic Growth, Education, and Environment, 2012, p. 24).

> From the moment I started working in the field of performance improvement, I set the Certified Performance Technologist designation as one of the milestones in my development path. Working with reputable practitioners inspired me to work even harder to apply global

best practices in the local context in Macedonia. Today, I can honestly say that having my CPT has helped me demonstrate the value I bring not only to the individuals and organizations I work with, but also to the sectors they operate in and society as a whole. Now as a fellow CPT dedicated to optimizing human potential within the work environment, I am proud to add to the practice by sharing a different perspective of using HPT in the developing world. (Maja Petkovska, CPT)

Regarding recertification, those who earn the CPT credential recertify every 3 years to demonstrate they are continuing to learn and grow through additional professional development and contributions to the performance improvement field.

Publishing is one of the most important aspects of expanding and advancing the field of performance improvement, and it is an opportunity for CPTs to earn points toward recertification. ISPI has five regular publications—each with a different purpose. Many CPTs contribute by writing case studies for its journal or books, such as the *Fundamentals of Performance Technology*, 3rd edition (Wiley, 2012). Case studies, in particular, gradually illustrate the vast situations where CPT standards are successfully applied. On a quarterly basis, the *CPT Update* highlights happenings in the CPT community, and a professional networking website, ISPI Collaborate, provides a platform for ongoing communication. In addition, ISPI's Awards of Excellence are based on the standards. Many times, a recipient of an award can use this as one of the projects in his or her CPT application or earn recertification points.

Founded in 1962, ISPI is the leading international association dedicated to improving productivity and performance in the workplace. ISPI represents performance improvement professionals throughout the United States, Canada, and more than 50 other countries. ISPI members are engaged in systematic inquiry of creating and measuring excellence at all levels:

- Work
- Worker
- Workplace
- World

Research-informed best practices are applied universally to pinpoint and address gaps in learning or to cultivate higher levels of achievement and performance within an organization. ISPI members work in a variety of industries worldwide and across all sectors, including business, nonprofit, government, academia, and armed forces. Ranks include performance improvement directors, human resources executives, e-learning specialists, organizational development directors, instructional designers, training directors, project managers, professors, consultants, and more.

ISPI's certification and accreditation programs give professionals and organizations a way to show they have both a commitment and proven capability to perform at the highest level. The Certified Performance Technologist (CPT) certification is a proficiency-based program for performance improvement and training professionals that validates their ability to produce results in the workplace. The CPT credential is global, flexible, accommodating to a variety of career paths, and based on a candidate's ability to boost performance under real-world conditions. The Certified School Improvement Specialist (CSIS) certification recognizes professionals who have demonstrated sustainable improvement in the performance of students, teachers, and school leaders. Accreditation recognizes a service, product, or course that meets a set of performance standards and code of ethics.

"This certification (CPT) provides practitioners of performance technology another means to validate their competence in the profession and be recognized for the value they have brought to the organizations they have served" (Rodger Stotz, CPT). "When CPT follows your name, it means you have produced quality work to specific standards. It announces your professional confidence to the world" (Carol Haig, CPT).

Microsoft

Historically, for some computer software applications, there was a misconception that some people who became trained were experts in the software. In fact, some people could pass the certification exam but did not have sufficient hands-on experience to fully understand the features and the complexities when some scenarios were encountered. These certified individuals became office workers or trainers on the applications, and it created a knowledge gap for software developers in the training space. Furthermore, numerous certifying bodies struggled with software training competency and worked hard to adapt the certification to real-life situations. Now, exams test much more than memorization of a concept or a software feature; many test business understanding and on-the-job scenarios. Microsoft, for example, has addressed software technical competency by segmenting the certification into two areas:

■ Information worker (IW): a person who uses Microsoft technology in his or her job and is considered a business professional
■ Information technology (IT) worker: an individual who is expected to have advanced expertise and may work in an IT department or as an IT professional

Microsoft Office Specialist (MOS) exams focus on the IW and are being managed through Certiport (http://www.certiport.com). Exams are given at an authorized testing center. All IT-type exams are managed through Microsoft and offered at an authorized testing center (e.g., Prometric). Both IW and IT exams provide levels that candidates can pursue based on their need for a short or long certification path. A credential earned could involve taking and passing one exam or taking and passing a number of different exams. The certification path can also map to a career path. This model is supported by other professional associations and professional organizations.

One of Microsoft's goals with respect to its current certification program is to help hiring managers determine who is qualified to perform specified job functions. The exams are designed to test hands-on experience, and exam questions are written to distinguish a new user from an experienced user. Earning a certification from Microsoft validates your knowledge and experience in a technology, and due to the ongoing rigor of the exams, this makes earning the credential a high value to both the individual and the organization.

My interview with Microsoft revealed some good things about their commitment to excellence:

Q: What were the first certifications offered, and what drivers led to those certifications being the first selected for implementation?

A: It began as Microsoft University in March 1992. Initial exams covered Windows 3.1, LAN Manager, and SQL Server. These were chosen because of IT Pro interest and need to get people trained on core technologies. Microsoft has instituted a number of high-quality options for their certification programs. The Microsoft IT Academy (ITA) offers a comprehensive approach to obtaining certification. Community colleges and 4-year universities have been well positioned to become Microsoft IT academies. Institutions with the Microsoft ITA name follow a defined curriculum. Interactive projects, participant collaboration, and online learning are some features of the Microsoft ITA curriculum.

Q: From an infrastructure standpoint, what does it require in terms of resources to support certification (i.e., which ones are the most challenging and why)?

A: This is multilayered. The support includes creating content that can be used in formal classroom training environments through our Microsoft Official Courseware (MOC) and Microsoft Official Academic Courseware (MOAC) in the academic space. The contents of this information typically are provided in concert with a formal training session via our Learning Partner channel or in an academic setting like our ITAs. We also have extensive training materials related to our exams that Microsoft Learning (MSL) offers online and through our Microsoft Press books. Beyond the creation and oversight of content, MSL provides extensive support, resources, and collateral to our Learning Partners and instructors, known as Microsoft certified trainers (MCTs). This includes training and marketing materials, special discounts and benefits, and overall channel support and administration. Microsoft has one of the most extensive and complete partner ecosystem support systems in the industry—if not the foremost—and that is continued in what MSL does with its Learning Partner channel. Other areas include exam verification to fight piracy and ensure Microsoft exams ensure those who pass are qualified in the technologies for which they have certifications. Microsoft has a very high standard for certification that requires rigor and oversight. They ensure the certifications continue to be valid and reliable from a statistical perspective, we do regular psychometric reviews; we engage industry subject matter experts (SMEs) to determine which skills are most important in the industry and are continually adding new questions within the content domains of the exams.

Q: What are some of the biggest challenges Microsoft has had to overcome to maintain high quality?

A: Challenges to maintaining quality come from many different places. It starts with the exam itself and ensuring that we're covering how Microsoft technologies are being used in the industry by our customers. To assist us with this, we engage industry SMEs throughout the development process, including writing the questions themselves. Those SMEs also help us identify the minimal skills and knowledge level that someone must be at in order to be minimally qualified to earn the certification. If this foundation for a quality exam isn't set, then the quality level will be compromised from the beginning. Once a quality exam is created, we then need to overcome issues with security and continued relevance of the exam. We work closely with our exam delivery provider to ensure our exam questions are protected, and that individuals testing are who they say we are. We also work with many other companies across the IT testing industry to educate on some of the fraudulent practices we see plaguing the industry so that our partners and customers are well informed and we can provide them with a fair learning and testing environment. Some tactics we use to protect the integrity of the exams include checking ID of candidates, including taking fingerprints and photos for some exams; adding new, innovative question types (less and less multiple choice) that are not easily memorized; performing data forensics or results analyses to find indicators of cheating; and closing test centers that are promoting or aiding candidates in cheating. Because we're regularly updating our certification exams, one additional area we have to pay particular attention to is ensuring our training materials continue to be relevant and are appropriately updated along with the exams. While we don't expect an individual to be able to pass our exams just by attending a training course, we do cover the same skills domains in each so that individuals can learn enough about the technology in the class that they can include hands-on experience with the technology and pass the exam.

Q: How are Microsoft certifications supported—when you think of professional associations, is it different for Microsoft as a professional organization?

A: At Microsoft, we have a community of Microsoft certified professionals, and Microsoft certifications are required to be part of the Microsoft Partner Network. In many ways, we act in a similar way to the professional associations/organizations in that we provide a body of knowledge for individuals as they prepare for earning a certification, we promote our certifications to the industry, and we build a community for certified individuals to engage with.

The subscription-based IT Academy program provides educators with professional development opportunities. To date, there are more than 10,000 IT Academy members in more than 160 countries. There are a significant number of high-technology resources available through the Microsoft IT Academy program, which gives educators the competitive advantage to remain current on the latest Microsoft technologies. This enables providers to easily integrate these technologies into curricula. With these resources, educators can customize courses to meet the needs of students of all ages and experience levels.

Microsoft continues to maintain high-quality certifications and has an excellent portfolio to support a career path for individuals:

■ Microsoft Certified Technology Specialist certifications
■ Microsoft Certified IT professional certification
■ Microsoft Certified Professional Developer certifications
■ Microsoft Certified Desktop Support Technician certifications
■ Microsoft Certified Solutions Expert

Project Management Institute

I had the pleasure of going to the Project Management Institute (PMI) in Newtown Square, Pennsylvania, in 2012 and met with Jim Snyder, one of the five founders of PMI. Since the founding of PMI in 1969, the organization, which worked out of Jim Snyder's home in Springfield, Pennsylvania, for its first 15 years, there has been an extraordinary growth of this professional association and the number of project management practitioners globally. In my opinion, Jim Snyder wins a professional association Emmy award for outstanding commitment.

Due to the extraordinary commitment of the professional staff and hundreds of volunteer members, PMI's far-reaching worldwide presence has encouraged the development of the project management profession and best practices. PMI is accredited by the ANSI as a standards developer. It has earned the distinction of being the first certification program to attain International Organization for Standardization (ISO) 9001 recognition. As of January 2013, PMI published the fifth edition of the *Project Management Body of Knowledge (PMBOK® Guide)* and updated numerous standards documents. PMI now offers seven different certification programs on a global basis:

- Certified Associate in Project Management (CAPM)
- PMI Agile Certified Practitioner (PMI-ACP)
- Program Management Professional (PgMP)
- Project Management Professional (PMP)
- PMI Risk Management Professional (PMI-RMP)
- PMI Scheduling Professional (PMI-SP)
- OPM3 (Organizational Project Management Maturity)

The most popular of the certification programs is the PMP. It requires five things:

1. Education (traditional 35 project management course hours)
2. Work experience hours totaling 4,500 (college degree) or 7,500 (high school education)
3. A passing grade on the PMP examination
4. Maintaining the credential through ongoing professional development units
5. Adherence to the PMP code of ethics

Dice.com rated the PMP certification as one of the most desirable certifications to obtain (Hill, 2012). The PMP certification is highly sought after in a number of disciplines, including IT. It was also perceived to be the highest-paying certification for 2013 (Muller, 2013). PMI published fact books in 1999 and 2001. Here are some highlights of the survey conducted by PMI:

Q: In the area of project management, are males or females more likely to pursue professional certification?

A: In 1999, PMI reported that 75% of PMPs were male.

Q: Are those with a college education more likely to pursue certification than those without a college education?

A: PMI reported 90% of those pursuing certification hold bachelor's or master's degrees.

Q: How many years of experience does the average certified project manager have?

A: PMI indicated that the average project manager has 12 years of experience.

Q: How long is the PMP exam?

A: There are 200 multiple-choice questions that are separated into five categories.

Q: Who publishes the standards documents for PMI?

A: PMI is fully staffed and publishes the standards documents.

The following are some of the updated statistics regarding PMI as of March 2013:

■ The number of total copies of the *PMBOK® Guide* was 4,020,301 (includes PMI-published translation).
■ PMI had 408,465 members.
■ There were 267 chapters.
■ There were 39 communities of practice.
■ PMP certification had been achieved by 516,229.
■ CAPM certification had been achieved by 20,447.
■ PMI-ACP had been achieved by 2,276.
■ PgMP certification had been achieved by 850.
■ Scheduling Professional (PMI-SP) certification had been achieved by 826.

An important component of growing membership is to customize programs to the needs and size of the audiences. PMI has done an outstanding job in this area:

■ PMI's corporate programs have been essential to growing large organization memberships.
■ The Registered Education Provider (REP) program has been established to ensure education providers meet or exceed established criteria and is available to companies as well as vendors. This enables some organizations to develop internal training programs.
■ Communities of practice represent an opportunity for members to focus on specific member requirements and interests. For example, PMI's legal community of practice is targeted toward those in the law profession and attracts attorneys, lawyers, paralegals, private investigators, and consultants to its forum.

The function of project management is unique in that it can be considered to be:

■ Interdisciplinary: within a discipline (i.e., legal cases)
■ Intradisciplinary: between disciplines (i.e., construction and hospitality)
■ Transdisciplinary: across disciplines (i.e., all occupations and industries)

Most people use project management in one form or another, and it can be thought of as a:

■ Function
■ Discipline
■ Profession
■ Role and responsibility

PMI has segmented project management into three domains:

■ **Project management:** Endeavors that are temporary, unique, and for a specific purpose to produce a product, service, or result.

■ **Program management:** The application of knowledge, skills, tools, and techniques to achieve the requirements for a program and realize increased benefits and improved control that might not be possible by managing related projects on an individual basis. It addresses the competing demands of cost, time, scope, resources, risk, and quality.

■ **Portfolio management:** The management and oversight of related projects and programs (portfolios) to ensure strategic objectives are met. Portfolio management goes to further lengths (when compared to program management) to deal with complexities, such as prioritization and competing demands due to the enormous tasks associated with portfolios.

What PMI has been able to accomplish since its foundation in the late 1960s is truly remarkable. A significant amount of the growth and development in project management can be directly or indirectly attributed to the efforts of PMI:

■ Emphasizing the need for professionalism and ethics in project management
■ The most comprehensive website in the world backed by the largest association staff focused on project management education and best practices
■ The largest producer of project management standards and literature
■ The largest support for collaboration and networking for project management professionals worldwide that has caused other organizations to increase their focus on how projects are managed
■ Competency models that identify knowledge, skills, and abilities in project management
■ Influencing the requirements for education and experience in project management as a prerequisite for employment
■ Specialized certificate programs in project management available from associations or organizations
■ Certificate programs in project management available from colleges and universities
■ Continuing education programs to support ongoing professional development in project management
■ Increasing membership size each year
■ Constant growth in the number of individuals becoming certified
■ Recognition of best-in-class certification by industry experts
■ Growth in publications from contributing authors
■ Enhanced business opportunities for vendors and suppliers who support PMI

Society of Human Resource Management

The Society of Human Resource Management (SHRM) is the professional largest association devoted to the management of human resources. SHRM continues to grow and now represents in excess of 250,000 members in more than 140 countries. SHRM was founded in 1948 and now has more than 575 affiliated chapters within the United States and subsidiary offices in China, India and United Arab Emirates. In my visit to SHRM headquarters in Alexandria, VA in 2012, I was impressed with the organization and commitment of its staff to association excellence. SHRM delivers quality on every level:

- Membership
- Certification resources and exam preparation materials
- Coordinated seamless support for numerous certification programs through the Human Resource Certification Institute (HRCI), a separate entity
- Research
- Publications
- Website
- Conferences
- Networking
- Resources such as templates and job aids that enable HR practitioners to do their job better
- Dispensing knowledge - advancing the profession of Human Resource Management through information sharing and communities of practice

SHRM has made new advances on a global basis as they have recently introduced the desired competencies for HR professionals. This was no small undertaking and required an extensive member survey, role delineation studies, job analyses, etc. to develop this new framework. Because SHRM's reach is world-wide, they are ideally positioned to address some very complex issues that organizations struggle with in the area of managing people. This includes, but is not limited to:

- Compensation
- Coaching and Mentoring
- Performance Evaluation
- Professional Development
- Compliance to policies and procedures
- Ethics
- Diversity
- Labor laws
- Mission, vision values
- Defining job descriptions and organizational structures
- Change management

- Tactical and strategic planning
- Career and succession planning
- This list is virtually endless due to HR being integrated into an organization's core functions

Suggested Reading

Hill, A. (2012). Be Certain. Retrieved September 14, 2012, from http://media.dice.com/report/certifications_contracting_pmp_itil_ccna/.

Half, R. (2013). Salary Guide for Technology Professionals: Cracking the Code for Technology Talent. Retrieved February 12, 2013, from http://www.roberthalftechnology.com/SalaryCenter.

Muller, R. (2013). 15 Top Paying Certifications for 2013. Retrieved February 5, 2013, from http://www.globalknowledge.com/training/generic.asp?pageid=3430&country=United+States.

Project Management Institute. (1999). *The PMI Project Management Fact Book.* Newtown Square, PA: Project Management Institute.

Project Management Institute. (2001). *The PMI Project Management Fact Book*, 2nd ed. Newtown Square, PA: Project Management Institute.

Resource CD

The resources provided on this CD are worth thousands of dollars and have taken a significant development effort. The tools support certification training and development. Resources are continuously updated and supported at http://certification-station.org. Some of the items included on the CD are:

- Compliance Advantage Learning Management System (CALMS): An MS Access database, fully editable (configurable) to meet requirements for tracking training
- Transferring Essential Lessons Learned (TELL) electronic board game
- Professional development unit/continuing education unit (PDU/CEU) tracker Microsoft Excel spreadsheet
- Training certificates' templates
- Training Resources and Information Library (TRAIL) , an MS Access database that enables you to catalog training and certification materials
- ROI Calculator
- Royalty free media kits
- Training aids
- Interactive exercises and games
- And more …

Acronyms

ABC: association of boards of certification
ABBT: Accrediting Board for Engineering and Technology
AMC: association management company
BOD: board of directors
BOK: body of knowledge
CA: credentialing authority
CDF: competency development framework
CP: certificate program
CSP: certification solutions provider
E&E: efficiency and effectiveness
HR: human resources
LMS: learning management system
NCCA: National Commission for Certifying Agencies
NOCA: National Association of Competency Assessment
PAM: professional association member
PCA: professional certification application
PCH: professional certification handbook
PCM: professional certification maintenance
PM: project management
REN: revised/enhanced/new (represent three approaches to changing a job description)
ROI: return on investment
ROQ: return on quality
SKATES: skills, knowledge, ability, talent, experience, sense
SO: sponsoring organization
TC&CC: technical colleges and community colleges
T&D: training and development

Glossary

Ability: Something the individual can perform physically or mentally (i.e., deal with ambiguity, fly on a plane, etc.).

Accountability: The degree to which an entity offering professional certification (i.e., professional organization or association) answers for its processes and procedures to stakeholders, including accrediting bodies, certificants, prospective certificants, boards of directors, and general public.

Accreditation: A time-limited and scope-defined recognition granted to an organization after verification indicates it has met specified criteria. It is a nongovernmental, voluntary process that evaluates institutions, agencies, and educational programs (i.e., institutions that grant certificates or diplomas). An organization grants public recognition to an entity (i.e., school, institute, college, university, or specialized program of study) for having met established standards as determined through initial and periodic evaluations. These evaluations may involve submitting a self-evaluation report, site inspection, and assessment by an independent board or commission.

Acculturation: A socialization process by which new or transferring workers become adjusted and part of the organization's culture. If an organization culture values certification, an individual will benefit politically by completing his or her certification.

Active Member: Member in current good standing in a professional association.

Advanced Degree: An advanced degree is at a level higher than a bachelor's degree. Advanced degrees include medical degrees, law degrees, master of science (MS), master of arts (MA), and doctoral (PhD) degrees from an institution of higher education.

Appropriateness: The degree to which a certification program fulfills the expectations of the occupation it targets or how relevant the certification program is to the job profile.

Assess: Evaluation for the purpose of understanding and describing the strengths and weaknesses of whatever is evaluated.

Assessment: The evaluation of achievement by administering a quiz or test (written or verbal) or skills inventory.

Background Check: The review of an individual's professional and personal information, which may include work experience, education, certifications, affiliations, licenses, criminal records, driving records, and so on.

Behavior Modeling: Trainees are given a demonstration of preferred attitudes and actions and then asked to follow this demonstration by emulating a similar approach. Those who become certified are frequently asked to serve as behavior models.

Benchmark: The quantifiable measurement of a best practice in a particular occupation. The benchmark becomes the standard against which others are measured.

Benefits: Indirect financial payments given to an employee, which may include items such as tuition or exam fee reimbursement for a certification program.

Bias: The tendency to discriminate against personal or professional characteristics, such as not being certified or licensed.

Biography: A summary document that provides a brief highlight of your prior work experience, education, and achievements. It should include certifications as appropriate.

Burden of Proof: Some applicants are audited during the process of obtaining certification when their application is processed. It is more likely that this happens when questions appear during certification review. While this is not always the case, it is helpful to create a checklist to ensure all required paperwork is handled correctly.

Bylaws: The bylaws of a professional association are core, common, and critical to the governance because they set forth the rules of operation (i.e., association's purpose, who can join, decision-making authority, etc.). Bylaws must allow for organizational change. Overly prescriptive bylaws are counterproductive.

Career Planning: A process of primarily five action steps—performance planning, development planning, coaching, compensation discussion, and performance evaluation. Performance planning concerns the roles and responsibilities of the employee, and may include stretch objectives, and integrates required job training that the employee needs to meet the agreed-on job requirements. Development planning encompasses the professional aspirations of the employee; it extends beyond required training and involves learning opportunities that are designed to help the employee exceed job requirements and grow to new levels. Coaching is an iterative process that reinforces job performance and encourages professional development. Compensation discussion is the financial reward that the employee realizes for his or her contribution. It is a combination of the employee's skills, knowledge, and abilities that intersects with the company's willingness to reward and recognize his or her contribution. Evaluation is the last step in the process that assesses the effectiveness and efficiency of the prior steps. It should look at performance, development, compensation, and coaching.

Case Study Method: The presentation of a scenario with a problem to solve. This serves as a practical method for developing employee training.

Central Tendency: A temptation to evaluate a group of employees the same way, avoiding high and the low ratings. Certification can help neutralize the central tendency by differentiating employees.

Certificant: Holder of a professional certification.

Certificate of Attendance: Verification an individual has attended assigned training sessions.

Certificate of Participation: Verification an individual was actively engaged in and attended assigned training sessions.

Certify: To confirm that a given set of circumstances has been met by an individual.

Certified: A person who has met the objectives of the certification.

Certification: The process by which an individual or group pursues acknowledgment, in which an association or organization grants recognition to a person, group, process, service, product, or result that meets or exceeds established criteria.

Certification Application: The documents required to apply for a professional certification.

Certification Renewal Fee: The periodic monetary payment required to maintain a certification. This periodic fee may be levied every 3 or 5 years or other designated interval. It is usually in addition to or separate from a membership fee.

Certification Examiner: An individual who reviews applicants who apply for a certification.

Certification Examiner Training: Training that individuals receive to prepare them for reviewing certification applications. Reviewers are usually certified themselves with the same certification or other certification offered by the professional association. This training usually encompasses how to utilize a checklist and prescribed template.

Certification Maintenance: The periodic education required to maintain certification. This may include attending chapter meetings, conferences, or related participation.

Certification Solutions Providers: Vendors who offer training products (i.e., flash cards) or services (i.e., instructor-led courses) to help people achieve or maintain their certifications. These are frequently packaged as PDUs or CEUs.

Civil Rights Act: This law states that it is illegal to discriminate in employment on the basis of race, color, religion, sex, or national origin. Therefore, every individual should be given equal access to training (i.e., obtaining certification).

Chapter Fees: Part of the membership fee a professional association may charge for local affiliation with a chapter of the parent organization.

Coaching: An interactive management and leadership approach that instills motivation and encouragement to help an individual realize his or her potential.

Code of Conduct: A written collection and understood set of rules, principles, values, behaviors, and relationships that a professional association will outline for adherence by those who become certified.

Community: A group of people who share similar interests (i.e., in a certification program).

Community Members: Certificants who belong to a professional organization.

Competency-Based Training: An educational process that focuses on specific knowledge, skills, and abilities that have been clearly defined and relate to the tasks currently being performed.

Conflict of Interest: A conflict of interest can occur when an individual or organization is involved in competing. For example, the salesperson has achieved two certifications. The certifications represented are from competing organizations, and the salesperson has to decide which one to represent. This person is given a special incentive to sell services from company A, when in fact company B is the better overall choice for the prospective customer. If the contract with the customer states that the customer will always be provided with the best solution from the vendor, then a conflict of interest may be occurring. First, the special incentive given may represent a conflict of interest, and not offering the best product under the circumstances can represent a conflict of interest.

Consideration: A state of reviewing an individual's education or experience for credentialing or certifying.

Consultant: A person or organization providing advice on products or services to an organization for specific purposes on a volunteer, contractual, or fee basis. Consultants may work on an hourly, daily, weekly, monthly, or project basis. They may also be paid a retainer for being available.

Content Validity: A test contains a representative sample of the tasks required on the job.

Continuing Education Unit (CEU): A measure of a training and development unit (usually hours) required of a certification program or licensed profession that is intended to keep the certified individual in the mindset of remaining up to date in career-related learning opportunities. Also known as professional development unit (PDU).

Credential: A credential is an attestation of competence or qualification issued to an individual or entity by a third-party credentialing authority (i.e., professional association).

Criteria: Operationally defined terms or statements used to clarify when an objective has been met or to evaluate the appropriateness of specific outcomes.

Criterion Validity: Proof that scores on the test are related to job performance.

Cross-Functional Team: A group of quality-focused individuals who have the desired competencies to work in more than one designated area (i.e., project management and supply chain management).

Culture: The attitudes, beliefs, and perspectives held by the organization. There are three types of organizational culture: bureaucratic, rules based, and learning. Each type of organizational culture will need certification.

Curriculum Vitae (CV): A curriculum vitae is a detailed description of work experience, education, and skills. It is generally more detailed than a résumé and is commonly used by those looking for an academic position (i.e., in an educational institution). A CV should include certifications obtained.

Degree Mill: An institution that issues certificates, certifications, licenses, degrees, or some other form of educational achievement without proper credentials. These entities create damage to professions by allowing entry of unqualified individuals into the field of practice.

Demonstration: The act of showing someone how to do something. In some cases, obtaining certification will require a demonstration.

Designation: Refers to the letters (or acronym) used after a name; for instance, John Doe, CSCP, refers to John Doe having earned the Certified Supply Chain Professional certification from Advancing Productivity Innovation and Competitive Success (APICS).

Development Planning: The process of reviewing the work-related activities, determining gaps, and then outlining opportunities for improvement while keeping in mind the aspirations of the individual.

Discrimination: The act of treating someone differently based on unspecified criteria or preference. If certification is required or desired in a position, then it should be listed. To deselect an individual because the person has not obtained a certification could be classified as discrimination.

Due Diligence: Acting responsibly and being accountable for a certain course of action (i.e., following up on a certification application after it has been submitted).

Education: The process of acquiring knowledge or skills required for a position.

Eligibility: The degree to which an individual meets or exceeds the requirements for certification.

Employee Satisfaction: The level of contentment that a colleague experiences with his or her job is many times contingent on factors such as development planning. A development plan can help an employee realize his or her potential. Certification can play a critical role in this process.

Empowerment: The realization by an individual that he or she can make decisions and accomplish specific goals without having to rely solely on another person or process.

Entity: Refers to an organization, business, or company that has received certification from a credentialing authority (i.e., a software developer certifies a company to deliver software training). The entity certified becomes responsible for certifying trainers to deliver the course.

Equal Pay Act of 1963: An amendment to the Fair Labor Standards Act that requires equal pay for women doing the same work as men. When a certification is issued, unless there are legal requirements or other rationale, the certification should be gender neutral.

Ethics: Principles, beliefs, or values that indicate whether an act is right or wrong. Most professional associations adhere to ethical codes that define standards of professional conduct.

Evaluation: The determination of merit (quality), value (worth), or significance (importance).

Examination: A process of determining if an individual has adequate understanding of subject matter. It usually consists of a series of questions that may be asked verbally or in writing, consisting of different types (i.e., multiple choice, true/false, yes/no, or select all that apply).

Exam Fee: The one-time charge associated with taking a test associated with a professional certification.

Experience: Observation or participation in an event that serves as a basis of knowledge.

Feedback: The mechanism of communication, verbal or written, to inform an individual how he or she is doing.

501(c)(3) Organization: The tax-exempt nonprofit organization status granted by the U.S. Internal Revenue Service (IRS).

Flex Time: The option to perform work at different intervals or time periods. There is a perception that those who become certified have more options to take advantage of positions that offer flex time.

For Profit: A business (professional organization) that intends to make a financial profit by offering certification products or services. These companies may provide services similar to those offered by professional associations, which may be classified as not for profit or nonprofit organizations.

Full-Time Education Status: A student classification that indicates the sole focus is education. The student may attend an educational institution at least 12 or 15 credit hours per semester. Generally, certification is typically regarded as part time or temporary and not full time.

Full-Time Equivalent (FTE): The hourly equivalent for a designated position can be one FTE employee at 40 hours per week, two employees at 20 hours per week, or four employees at 10 hours per week.

Globalization: The extension of human resources to other locations worldwide.

Goals: Objectives, targets, and plans that you hope to achieve given anticipated conditions. Goals are most powerful when they are regularly reviewed. Goals that include professional development (i.e., certification) need to have a schedule to ensure conformance. To this end, an accountability study partner may be required for some certifications.

Governance: Management and leadership of an organization responsible for administrative operational functions, including but not limited to financials, customer service, and membership relations.

Governing Body: An entity that has the legal authority or jurisdiction to establish policies and procedures and provide oversight to promote quality and ensure compliance of operations.

Grandfathered: To be covered due to a preexisting condition. Those who obtain a certification are given certain privileges based on holding a certain level of experience, education, or other certification.

Grievance: Formal complaint against a professional organization or association for the purpose of bringing public awareness in hopes for a change or resolution. This usually involves legal action.

Halo Effect: In a performance evaluation, a supervisor's rating of a subordinate on one strong trait (usually positive) biases the rating of that person on other traits. Those who become certified need to be conscious of the halo effect.

Human Capital: Competency stock of the individuals who work for the organization.

Human Resource Development: The framework for helping employees realize and develop their skills, talents, knowledge, and abilities. It includes training, performance management, coaching, mentoring, shadowing, career and succession planning, and related organization development.

Human Resource Management: The oversight and related staffing functions required to ensure the effective and efficient management of people (i.e., full time, part time, temporary, seasonal) designated as employees/colleagues/members (internal) and in some cases contractors/consultants (external) to meet the performing organization's needs. It includes the related processes of screening, recruiting, orienting, training, compensating, rewarding, appraising, and developing.

Illegal Tying Arrangement: Mandating that an individual is a member of a professional association in order to maintain professional certification when, in fact, it is not a requirement.

Implementability: Refers to the ability to implement a program with consideration to risk and reward.

Independent Contractor: A person who is independently employed and contracts with a professional organization or association on a part-time or full-time basis, such as a trainer for a certification program.

Integrity: The value that must be withheld after obtaining a certification as it applies to representation in personal and professional communication.

Interview: The process of identification and possible selection of an individual (i.e., employee, contractor, consultant, vendor).

Job Analysis: The comprehensive assessment of the position description, which may include a decomposition of the work performed on the job. It involves training and development, recruitment, compensation, performance evaluation, and development planning.

Job Benchmarking: A technique to determine the employee's pay scale by comparing similar jobs with respect to relative worth.

Job Description: A list of a tasks, duties, roles, responsibilities, supervisory responsibilities, reporting relationships, and working conditions a person is required to fulfill to meet expectations.

Job Fit: The alignment of the roles, responsibilities, and expectations of the job to skills, knowledge, and aspirations of the individual.

Job Grade: A job classification system that determines the relative level of a position (i.e., supervisor, manager, director, vice president, etc.).

Job Posting: The listing of a position of employment internally or externally through various means.

Job Sharing: A job-splitting concept that allows two to more people to share a position, usually a single full-time role and responsibility.

Knowledge Management: The systematic collection and synthesis of data and information to support understanding in decision making. Certification should support higher-level thinking in knowledge management.

Layoff: An employment situation in which there is a shortage of work for an employee, or the current employee does not have the desired skills to perform the designated work available. Certification becomes a desirable option for corrective action and employee retraining.

Learning Organization: An organization that proposes to adapt to change, embrace continuous improvement, and remain flexible as demands for their products and services evolve.

Liability: Obligation or responsibility.

Licensure: Licensure is an involuntary process by which a government agency regulates an occupation. It grants permission to an individual to engage in a job if it finds that the individual has attained the degree of competency required to ensure health, safety, and welfare will be protected. Licensing is based on the action of a legislative body. Once a licensing law has been passed, it becomes against the law for an individual to engage in that occupation unless the person has a license.

Lifetime Certification: Individuals who have retired from a profession and have been certified for a specified number of years may be eligible for this status. The purpose of lifetime certification is to acknowledge accomplishments and retain membership. By retaining lifetime members, a professional association is able to engage these individuals as active members to serve on boards, write articles, and so on.

Malcolm Baldrige Award: A quality-focused award created by the U.S. Department of Commerce that recognizes U.S. companies. This certification is rigorous and thorough.

Mandatory Professional Certification: Professional certification that is required of a profession.

Membership Dues: Fees associated with belonging to a professional association; they are usually assessed on an annual basis.

Mentoring: To remain empathetic while remaining a role model with the goal of succession planning in mind.

Message Clusters: Body language is classified in message clusters, such as relaxed, submissive, bored, aggressive, or defensive. These are important to control during phases of verbal examinations during the certification process.

Monitoring: The act of continuously reviewing a certification program to ensure quality and compliance.

Needs Assessment: A preevaluation that is conducted to determine requirements for a program.

Networking: The process of meeting with individuals on a periodic basis to support best practices, benchmarking, and job referrals.

Not for Profit: An organization that proposes to be charitable or benevolent rather than turning a profit. Not-for-profit organizations are often given special tax treatment.

Objective: A job requirement.

OJT: On-the-job training that occurs in a structured format, usually involving a trainer.

Oral Exam: A quiz or test that is delivered verbally by an individual or group. The respondent may be required to respond in a spoken or written manner.

Organization: Company, business, firm, institution, entity, and so on that is composed of two or more individuals, employs people, and conducts or is involved in business-related transactions.

Outplacement Counseling: The process of helping a terminated employee understand his or her options for future employment elsewhere. Certification becomes a key consideration in this process.

Outsourcing: Acquiring resources outside the performing organization; is sometimes due to the expertise required.

Panel Interview: A candidate interview for a position that is performed by a group of individuals.

Performance Appraisal: A critical review of the completion of work-related objectives. This is typically performed at the end of the project or on an annual basis.

Points: The unit of measure for achieving or maintaining certification in PDUs/CEUs.

Professional Association: A professional association is sometimes referred to as a body, organization, or society. It is nonprofit in nature. A nonprofit status is not a legal or technical definition. It basically refers to a professional association that uses surplus revenues to achieve its objectives rather than to distribute them as profit or dividends to stakeholders, in this case members of the professional association.

Professional Development Day (PDD): Series of speaking events that are coordinated over a period of one full day to help certificants earn PDUs/CEUs.

Professional Development Unit (PDU): A measure of a training and development unit (usually hours) required of a certification program or licensed profession that is intended to keep the certified individual in the mindset of remaining up to date in career-related learning opportunities. Also known as a continuing education unit (CEU).

Professionalization: Formalized achievement associated with obtaining a certification. This includes building a framework by which an individual can be regarded as a professional with the certification.

Promotion: The advancement of an individual due to work performance. Sometimes, educational achievement or certification plays a role in this process.

Protocol: The recommended way to address something or interact with others.

Qualified: An individual who meets specified requirements (i.e., of education, experience, credentials, or certification).

Qualifications: The accomplishments of an individual with respect to education, work experience, or other criteria.

Qualify: Meeting the minimum specified criteria as outlined in the requirements specification.

Quality: Defines the desirable attributes of a product, a process, or a service meeting or exceeding stated expectations.

Questionnaire: The written or verbal instrument used to inquire of an individual (i.e., for employment or engagement).

Recertification: The periodic requirement of meeting existing or new objectives for certification or licensure.

Reference Letter: The document that serves to verify an individual carried out his or her work responsibilities to the satisfaction of the employer, and the person could be recommended to someone else for a similar assignment. Reference letters are sometimes required for certification.

Reliability: Consistency of scores obtained by the same person or group of people provided with the same training and when retested with equivalent test instruments.

Remediation: Steps to correct something that is in error.

Renewal: The period of time slated for reestablishing a certification (i.e., every 3 years).

Resource: People (i.e., full-time employee, part-time contractor, consultant, vendor, supplier); system (i.e., hardware, software); facilities (i.e., meeting rooms); equipment (i.e., machine or tool); material (i.e., training manuals); or supplies (i.e., copy paper).

Review Interval: The date a policy, procedure, or other document needs to be reread to ensure knowledge is retained.

Résumé: A comprehensive document that provides a detailed outline of a person's prior work experience, education, and achievements.

Revoke: Cancel or suspend a certification for reasons pertaining to not adhering to standards.

Role-Playing: Individuals create a realistic environment and situation that may occur in the future and act it out in hopes of being able to prepare proactively for a future occurrence.

Rubric: A set of criteria used for assessing a job or performance in a job. A rubric usually includes levels of performance for each established criterion.

Shadowing: Following a peer, mentor, or coach for the purpose of seeing how the person performs a task.

Simulated Learning (Work) Environment: Work locations that offer structured off-the-job training (i.e., off-line equipment).

Smart Objective: Objective that is specific, measurable, achievable, realistic, and timely.

Social Media: The tools and platforms used to publish content online. It is frequently used for networking purposes.

Sponsor: The individual who supports the professional certification by allowing for the investment of time or money (i.e., pays annual membership dues in a professional association).

Sponsoring Organization: The company that supports the professional certification by allowing for the investment of time or money (i.e., pays annual membership dues in a professional association). The sponsoring organization may serve in other capacities, such as allowing for the assembly of a study group to support professional certification. In this instance, the organization is donating its facilities to support professional certification.

Stakeholder: A person with a vested interest in something (i.e., employer, certificant, sponsor, vendor, etc.).

Stressor: A circumstance, issue, person, or anything that contributes to stress or mental or emotional discomfort.

Stretch Objective: An objective that has an extension. It is frequently perceived as top performance or overperformance or exceeds expectation.

Study Group: A periodic meeting of individuals (weekly or biweekly) to review subject matter pertaining to professional development as outlined by the professional association, which usually intends to help individuals achieve or maintain certification.

Succession Planning: Preparing for those who will assume responsibility in the future.

Termination: The voluntary or involuntary end of a program or position.

Test Validity: The accuracy with which an assessment, quiz, test, and so on purports to measure.

Triple E: Education, experience, and employment, which usually represent the three most common variables reviewed to award professional certification.

Tuition Assistance: A discretionary, employer-provided reimbursement for educational programs (i.e., certification training programs).

Usefulness: The practicality and transferability of education or certification to the workplace.

Values: Items, actions, feelings (e.g., integrity) held true by a group of people.

Voluntary Professional Certification: Professional certifications that are optional and not required of a profession.

Volunteer: Someone who freely gives of time and energy for the purpose of advancing a cause.

Work Samples: Examples of complete work (i.e., templates produced, presentations designed, or training programs created).

Written Exam: A test taken by hand or electronically that has a series of questions in various formats (true/false, yes/no, multiple choice, select all that apply, fill in the blank, drag and drop, etc.).

References

Answers.com. (2010). What is the average time it takes to read aloud one full page of text? Retrieved on June 15, 2012. from http://wiki.answers.com/Q/What_is_the_average_time_it_takes_to_read_aloud_one_full_page_of_text.

ASAE and the Center for Association Leadership. (2006). *7 Measures of Success: What Remarkable Associations Do that Others Don't.* American Management Press. Alexandria, VA: ASAE.

Barnhart, P. (1997). *The Guide to National Professional Certification Programs,* 2nd ed. Boca Raton, FL: CRC Press and Amherst, MA: HRD Press.

Brinkerhoff, R. (2006). *Telling training's story. Evaluation made simple, credible, and effective.* San Francisco: Berrett-Koehler Publishers.

Calwen, F. (2013). Phone interview conducted on February 6, 2013 regarding e-learning development.

Canadian Information Center for International Certification. (n.d.). General Guiding Principles for Good Practice in the Assessment of Foreign Credentials. Retrieved February 4, 2013, from http://www.cicic.ca/502/good-practice.canada.

Christianson, J., and Fajen, A. (1998). *Computer and Network Professional's Certification Guide.* New York: Sybex.

Collett, M. (2007). Guide to Professional Qualifications. Retrieved February 1, 2001, from http://www.jobs.ac.uk/careers-advice/careers-advice/947/guide-to-professional-qualifications.

Dalton, J., and Dignam, M. (2007). *The Decision to Join: How Individuals Determine Value and Why They Choose to Belong.* Washington, DC: ASAE and the Center for Association Leadership.

Fine, S., and Getkate, M. (1995). *Benchmark Tasks for Job Analysis: A Guide for Functional Job Analysis (FJA) Scales.* Mahwah, NJ: Erlbaum.

Grettenberger, J. (2013). *Five Tips to Get IT Auditors Off Your Back.* White paper. Aliso Viejo, CA: Dell Software.

Hale, J. (2002). *Performance-based evaluation: Tools and techniques to measure the impact on training.* Pfeiffer.

Hale, J. (2012). Performance-based certification: How to design a valid, defensible, cost-effective program, 2nd ed. Pfeiffer.

Hill, A. (2012). Be Certain. Retrieved September 14, 2012, from http://media.dice.com/report/certifications_contracting_pmp_itil_ccna/.

Kinglsey, J. (2013). Phone interview conducted on March 16, 2013 pertaining to creating assessments for e-learning.

Knapp & Associates International. (2007). *Knapp Certification Industry Scan*. Princeton, NJ: Knapp International.

Manijack, P. (n.d.). Qualification versus certification. *Certification Magazine*. Retrieved February 1, 2013, from http://www.certmag.com/read.php?in=773.

Marquardt, M. (1996). *Building the Learning Organization*. New York: McGraw Hill.

Muller, R. (2013). 15 Top Paying Certifications for 2013. Retrieved February 5, 2013, from http://www.globalknowledge.com/training/generic.asp?pageid=3430&country=United+States/.

Project Management Institute. (2013). *A Guide to the Project Management Body of Knowledge*, 5th ed.). Newtown Square: PA: Project Management Institute.

Senge, P. (1994). *The Fifth Discipline Fieldbook: Strategies and Tools for Building a Learning Organization*. New York: Crown Business.

Tittel, E (2003). *IT Certification Success*. Indianapolis, IN: Que.

U.S. Agency for International Development (USAID) Bureau for Economic Growth, Education, and Environment. (2012). Human and Institutional Capacity Development for Non-Critical Priority Countries (HICDpro for Non-CPCs). Retrieved from https://www.fbo.gov.

Wyrostek, W.E. (2008). *The Top 10 Problems with IT Certification in 2008*. Indianapolis, IN: Cisco Press. Retrieved from http://www.ciscopress.com/articles/article.asp?p=1180991.

Additional Reading

Basarab, D. (1990). Calculating the return on training investment. *American Journal of Evaluation* 11, 177–185.

Bogardus, A. (2009). *PHR/SPHR Professional in Human Resources Certification Study Guide*. New York: Sybex.

Case, S.M., and Swanson, D.B. (1998). Constructing written test questions for the basic and clinical sciences.

Cizek, G. (2007). *Standard Setting: A Guide to Establishing and Evaluating Performance Standards on Tests*. Thousand Oaks, CA: Sage.

Coers, M., Gardner, C., Higgins, L., and Raybourn, C. (2001). *Benchmarking—A Guide for Your Journey to Best-Practice Processes*. Houston, TX: APQC.

Damelio, R. (1995). *The Basics of Benchmarking*. Portland, OR: Productivity Press.

Davidson, J. (2005). *Evaluation Methodology Basics: The Nuts and Bolts of Sound Evaluation*. Thousand Oaks, CA: Sage.

Dhanens, V. (1984). Evaluation of instructor performance. *American Journal of Evaluation* 5, 37–40.

Durley, C. (2005). *The NOCA Guide to Understanding Credentialing Concepts*. Washington, DC: National Organization for Competency Assurance.

Edwards, J., Scott, J., and Raju, N. (2003). *The Human Resources Program-Evaluation Handbook*. Thousand Oaks, CA: Sage.

Heldman, K. (2005). *Project Management Professional Study Guide*, 4th ed. Hoboken, NJ: Wiley.

Ingram, R. (2009). *Ten Basic Responsibilities of Nonprofit Boards*, 2nd ed. (BoardSource). Retrieved January 2, 2012, from http://www.boardsource.org/Knowledge.asp?ID=3.368.

Kasar, J., and Clark, E. (2000). *Developing Professional Behaviors*. Thorofare, NJ: Slack.

Kurpius, S., and Stafford, M. (2006). *Testing and Measurement: A User-Friendly Guide.* Thousand Oaks, CA: Sage.

Newell, S., and Swan, J. (2000). Trust and inter-organizational networking. *Human Relations* 53(10), 1287–1328.

Ory, J., and Ryan, K. (1993). *Tips for Improving Testing and Grading,* Vol 4. Newbury Park, CA: Sage.

Phillips, J., and Phillips, P. (2002). Technology's return on investment. *Advances in Developing Human Resources* 4, 512–532.

Project Management Institute. (2002). *Project Manager Competency Development Framework.* Newtown Square: PA: Project Management Institute.

Project Management Institute. (2007). Source: Project Management Institute Code of Ethics and Professional Conduct. Retrieved July 17, 2007, from http://www.pmi.org/PDF/ap_pmicodeofethics.pdf.

Reider, R. (2000). *Benchmarking Strategies: A Tool for Profit Improvement.* Hoboken, NJ: Wiley.

Smith, M. (1999). Should AEA begin a process for restricting membership in the profession of evaluation? *American Journal of Evaluation* 22, 281–300.

Stewart, B. (2013). Rule of thumb (Heuristic).

Index

About the Author

Willis H. Thomas, PhD, PMP, CPT is a certified project manager and performance Technologist who has been involved in training and organizational development across the pharmaceutical, telecommunications and information technology industries. His career focus has been in the areas of Quality Assurance, Human Resources and Operations.

Dr. Thomas is a recognized author. His book entitled *"The Basics of Project Evaluation and Lessons Learned"* received the Project Management Institute 2012 Cleland Award. The Cleland award recognizes and honors the best project management literature published during the previous calendar year. It recognizes the author for significant contributions and for advancing the project management knowledge, practices, procedures, concepts, or other advanced techniques that demonstrate the value of using project management. He has also published in professional journals and is represented on training, project management and evaluation professional association websites. He was a featured speaker at the International Project Management Day on November 15, 2012 and has delivered global presentations on project management, training and evaluation for a number of organizations.

Dr. Thomas has 10 years of pharmaceutical experience. He worked for Pfizer in Kalamazoo, MI, the largest manufacturing site for Drug Products and Active Pharmaceutical Ingredients. After the Wyeth-Pfizer merger, he worked five years in Research and Development in Pearl River, NY. Dr. Thomas' work has been instrumental in maintaining regulatory compliance (i.e., with the FDA) and supporting process improvement (i.e., through assessing and developing global training programs). In addition to a deep and broad experience in the pharmaceutical industry, Dr. Thomas was in the telecommunications and information technology industries for 15 years where he supported quality initiatives and regulatory compliance. He worked seven years for Ameritech, a Regional Bell Operating Company (RBOC);

three years for Brinks, an international home security provider; and five years for Presentation Partners as a consultant.

In the area of project management training, Dr. Thomas has delivered courses on a virtual basis for the International Institute for Learning. He has also invested time to assist a number of professional associations with learning technologies, project management and evaluation. He has done this through creating e-learning, delivering webinars, in-person speaking engagements and publishing content.

He holds a PhD in Evaluation from Western Michigan University. The title of his dissertation while working at Pfizer was "A Metaevaluation of Lessons Learned Repositories: Evaluative Knowledge Management Practices in Project Management." In line with his extensive research, he has developed a comprehensive website on project management that focuses specifically on lessons learned at www.lessonslearned.info. Dr. Thomas studied directly under Dr. Michael Scriven. His Master of Science degree in Human Resource Management is from National Louis University. The title of his Master's thesis was "The Impacts of Sales Integration on Integration on Interpersonal Communication Affecting Sales Representatives Job Satisfaction." This was completed while at Xerox.

Dr. Thomas' Bachelor of Arts degree is from the University of Wisconsin-Madison. While there, he served as the editor for Datelines Student Newspaper and editor for West African Monsoons from Geocentric Satellites (Space Science and Engineering Department).

Personal Interests: Family, travel, visiting national parks, gourmet cooking and publishing Professional Interests: Evaluation, Measurement, Research, Certification Programs, Learning Technologies, Pharmaceutical Science, Project Management, Supply Chain Management, Records Management, Information Technology, Information Management, and Knowledge Management Professional Association Board of Directors Served on: ASTD, APICS, PMI, and ISM Current Professional Memberships: AEA, APICS, ASTD, ISPI, and PMI